The Return of Depression Economics

PAUL KRUGMAN

The Return of Depression Economics

ALLEN LANE
THE PENGUIN PRESS

ALLEN LANE
THE PENGUIN PRESS

Published by the Penguin Group
Penguin Books Ltd, 27 Wrights Lane, London w8 5tz, England
Penguin Putnam Inc., 375 Hudson Street, New York, New York 10014, USA
Penguin Books Australia Ltd, Ringwood, Victoria, Australia
Penguin Books Canada Ltd, 10 Alcorn Avenue, Toronto, Ontario, Canada m4v 3b2
Penguin Books (NZ) Ltd, Private Bag 102902, NSMC, Auckland, New Zealand

Penguin Books Ltd, Registered Offices: Harmondsworth, Middlesex, England

First published in the USA by W. W. Norton & Company Inc. 1999
First published in Great Britain by Allen Lane The Penguin Press 1999
1 3 5 7 9 10 8 6 4 2

Copyright © Paul Krugman, 1999
All rights reserved

The moral right of the author has been asserted

Printed in Great Britain by The Bath Press, Bath

A CIP catalogue record for this book is available from the British Library

ISBN 0–713–99389–8

Contents

CONTENTS

Introduction

OST economists, to the extent that they think about the subject at all, regard the Great Depression of the 1930s as a gratuitous, unnecessary tragedy. If only Herbert Hoover hadn't tried to balance the budget in the face of an economic slump; if only the Federal Reserve hadn't defended the gold standard at the expense of the domestic economy; if only officials had rushed cash to threatened banks, and thus calmed the bank panic that developed in 1930–31; then the stock market crash of 1929 would have led only to a garden-variety recession, soon forgotten. And since economists and policymakers have learned their lesson—no modern treasury secretary would echo Andrew Mellon's famous advice to "liquidate labor, liquidate stocks, liquidate the farmers, liquidate real estate . . . purge the rottenness out of the system"—nothing like the Great Depression can ever happen again.

Or can it? Over the course of the last two years seven economies—economies that still produce about a quarter of the world's output and that are home to two-thirds of a billion people—have experienced an economic slump that bears an eerie resemblance to the Great Depression. Now as then the crisis has struck out of a clear blue sky, with most pundits predicting a continuing boom even as the slump gathered momentum; now as then the conventional economic medicine has proved ineffective, perhaps even counterproductive. True, with the exception of Indonesia none of the afflicted economies has suffered a truly Depression-level decline in output; and though ripples from the storm have threatened to capsize national economies from South Africa to Argentina, the world economy as a whole has nonetheless continued to grow. But while things could have been (and still could get) worse, the fact that something like this could happen at all in the modern world should send chills up the spine of anyone with a sense of history.

Of course, this is not the first world economic crisis since the 1930s. Measured by their overall impact on gross world product, the two energy crises—the global recessions that followed the Yom Kippur War of 1973, and the Iranian revolution of 1979— were worse than the financial crisis of the late nineties, because unlike the recent events they produced recessions in Europe and America. Individual countries and regions have also had their travails: in particular, Latin America took more than seven years to work its way out of the debt crisis that began in 1982. But these earlier crises, terrible as they were for their victims, were in a way less troubling than what has happened in the last two years, because they were not so seemingly gratuitous. One might ask why the real price of oil doubled after 1973, and doubled again after 1979; but whatever the reasons for a global oil shortage, given the existence of such a shortage, a global recession was not too surprising. One might ask why banks were willing to lend Latin American countries so much money in the 1970s, and why the money was used so badly; but given the "debt overhang" that resulted, a prolonged and painful economic slump was only to be expected. Up to now, in other words, major economic crises have had correspondingly major causes.

But what has caused Japan—that feared economic power-

Introduction

house of the 1980s—to spend most of this decade in near-stag-
nation and recently to go into a deflationary tailspin? How did
a few bad real estate loans and a botched devaluation in Thailand—a small, faraway country of which most people knew
nothing—set dominoes toppling from Indonesia to South
Korea? Why did a debt default by Russia—a former military
superpower, but nowadays an economic midget—lead to economic disaster in Brazil and for a few, terrifying weeks cause the
U.S. bond market to "freeze up"? In each case the effect, the
damage done, seems vastly disproportionate to the cause—capital (capital market?) punishment imposed on economies guilty
of nothing more than financial misdemeanors.

Moreover, the kind of economic trouble that the world has
recently suffered is precisely the sort of thing we thought we
had learned to prevent. In the bad old days big, advanced
economies with stable governments—like Britain in the
1920s—might have had no answer to prolonged periods of stagnation and deflation; but between John Maynard Keynes and
Milton Friedman, we thought we knew enough to keep that
from happening again. Smaller countries—like Austria in
1931—may once have been at the mercy of financial tides,
unable to control their economic destiny; but nowadays sophisticated bankers and government officials (not to mention the
International Monetary Fund) are supposed to quickly orches-
trate rescue packages that contain such crises before they
spread. Governments—like that of the United States in
1930–31—may once have stood by helplessly as national banking systems collapsed; but in the modern world deposit insurance and the readiness of the Federal Reserve to rush cash to
threatened institutions are supposed to prevent such scenes. No
sensible person thought that the age of economic anxiety was
past; but whatever problems we might have in the future, we
were sure that they would bear little resemblance to those of
the 1920s and 1930s.

And then came the latest crisis. The truth is that Japan has
been bearing a growing resemblance to a 1930s economy since

the early years of this decade; but only in the last couple of years has it become clear that the country is stuck in a trap that Keynes and his contemporaries would have found completely familiar. The smaller economies of Asia, by contrast, went from boom to calamity virtually overnight—and the story of their downfall reads as if it were taken straight out of a financial history of the 1930s. And for a few weeks in 1998 the United States experienced what was for all practical purposes a classic bank run, except that it did not involve any institutions called banks. Suddenly, it seems, everything old is new again.

Think of it this way: it is as if bacteria that used to cause deadly plagues, but that have long been considered conquered by modern medicine, were to reemerge in a form resistant to all the standard antibiotics. So far only a limited number of people have actually fallen prey to the newly incurable strains; but even those of us who have so far been lucky would be foolish not to seek new cures, new prophylactic regimens, whatever it takes, lest we turn out to be the next victims. And to do that we must first try to understand how so much can have gone wrong for so many economies.

That is the purpose of this volume. It is a short book, produced in mid-crisis; at the time of writing (January 1999) emerging Asia seemed to have won its way back to precarious stability, but Brazil was going over the edge, and every week brought fresh bad news from Japan. Eventually there will be longer and more thorough books, written with the benefit of hindsight. In the long run we will understand, better than anyone can at the moment, how we got into this mess, and what can be done to prevent similar messes in the future. But, as Keynes famously put it, in the long run we are all dead. How did this crisis happen? How can we turn it around and prevent it from spreading? These are questions that demand immediate answers, even if we know that those answers are at best provisional and that some of what we say now will surely look silly in five or ten years.

The subject of this book is so new—the "hot" phase of the crisis began only with the devaluation of Thailand's baht in July

1997—that the phenomenon has not even acquired a generally accepted name. In the early stages a variety of disease metaphors were suggested: the "Asian flu," the "Asian contagion," "bahtulism" (my own contribution). But it has gradually become clear that while the damage has been concentrated in Asia (so far), this is not merely a story about Asia: if something like this could happen to countries that the World Bank described in 1993 as paragons of "pragmatic orthodoxy," which had been "remarkably successful in creating and sustaining macroeconomic stability," who knows which country may be next? It is sometimes referred to as the "emerging market crisis"; but Japan, which has about twice as large an economy as all the rest of the afflicted countries put together, has long since "emerged." George Soros's book from last fall was entitled *The World Financial Crisis* (published in the U.K. as *The Crisis of Global Capitalism*); but these events have gone far beyond financial markets per se, and even when or if financial markets calm down, the real effects of the crisis—the damage to growth, employment, and the standard of living—will linger on.

I hereby propose another name: the Great Recession. I call it a "recession" rather than a depression because, catastrophic as the last two years have been for some countries, at a global level the damage has so far been well short of Depression levels (cross your fingers). But it deserves the honorific "great," because for the afflicted countries it has indeed been the worst (economic) thing they have experienced in half a century. And the allusion to the Great Depression seems to me entirely appropriate: as Mark Twain might have said, recent events may not have repeated those of the 1930s, but they do rhyme.

About This Book

Let me admit at the outset that this book is, at bottom, an analytical tract. It is not so much about *what* happened as *why* it happened; the important things to understand, I believe, are how this catastrophe can have happened, how the victims can recover, and how we can prevent it from happening again. This means that the ultimate objective is, as they say in business schools, to develop the theory of the case—to figure out how to think about this stuff.

But I have tried to avoid making this a dry theoretical exposition. There are no equations, no inscrutable diagrams, and (I hope) no impenetrable jargon. As an economist in good standing, I am quite capable of writing things nobody can read. Indeed, unreadable writing—my own and others'—played a key role in helping me arrive at the views presented here. But what the world needs now is informed action; and to get that kind of action, ideas must be presented in a way that is accessible to concerned people at large, not just those with economics Ph.D.'s. Anyway, the equations and diagrams of formal economics are, more often than not, no more than a scaffolding used to help construct an intellectual edifice. Once that edifice has been built to a certain point, the scaffolding can be stripped away, leaving only plain English behind.

It also turns out that although the ultimate goal here is analytical, much of the writing involves narrative. Partly this is because the story line—the sequence in which events happened—is often an important clue to what theory of the case makes sense. (For example, any "fundamentalist" view of economic crisis—that is, a view that economies only get the punishment they deserve—must come to grips with the peculiar coincidence that so many seemingly disparate economies hit the wall in the space of a few months.) But I am also aware that the story line provides a necessary context for any attempts at explanation and that most people have not spent the last eighteen months obsessively following the unfolding drama. Not everyone recalls what Prime Minister Mahathir said in Kuala Lumpur in August 1997 and relates it to what Donald Tsang ended up doing in Hong Kong a year later; well, this book will refresh your memory.

Finally, in writing this book, I have tried to resist four intellectual seductions that I believe have marred much of the ongoing discussion of recent events

The first is the seduction of twenty-twenty hindsight: now

that we know that Japan and Korea have experienced a devastating economic setback, we start to imagine that we always knew that they had feet of clay. We forget the astonishment we first felt when these paragons began to lose their way, an astonishment that was in fact entirely appropriate, because it is by no means obvious even now how things can have gone so wrong. And associated with the seduction of hindsight is the temptation to engage in fatalism: knowing as we do that Japan is in trouble now, we start to regard that trouble as inevitable, with deep roots reaching all the way back to the Meiji Restoration — and dismiss as naive the idea that there might be any quick fix. Well, maybe — but maybe the problem is less fundamental than that, and there really is a quick fix after all; the point is that this is a question to be answered only after hard thinking.

Second, as I mentioned earlier, there is a temptation to think of this as purely an *Asian* crisis. Not very long ago there were many pundits, Western as well as Asian, who claimed that an "Asian miracle," based on a superior "Asian system" and underpinned by uniquely superior "Asian values," ensured that the boom in Asia would go on for the foreseeable future, untroubled by Western-style slumps. Now many pundits — in many cases the same pundits! — insist that the crisis was an inevitable consequence of the unique failings of the Asian system. But if the system was so flawed, why did it work so well for so long, then fail so suddenly? And how can we be sure that next year, or the year after, our own system may not turn out to have hidden flaws, that we ourselves may not be vulnerable to crisis? (Indeed, as we will see, the U.S. economy actually *did* come dangerously close to catastrophe in the fall of 1998.) Again, we should approach the question with an open mind, not simply stand our previous Asia worship on its head.

Third, a somewhat related danger, is the inclination to moralize. Nobody seems to know who coined the phrase "crony capitalism," but it certainly corresponds to a real phenomenon in Asia before the crisis. To conclude, however, that this cronyism was the sole cause of crisis, to assert without solid evidence that the crisis was simply the wages of sin, is premature — and is surely tempting fate. Judge not, lest you yourself be judged, and maybe sooner than you think.

Finally, one temptation that often afflicts writers on economics, especially when the subject is so grave, is the tendency to become excessively dignified. Not that the events we are concerned with aren't important, in some cases matters of life and death. Too often, though, pundits imagine that because the subject is serious, it must be approached solemnly: that because these are big issues, they must be addressed with big words; no informality or levity allowed. As it turns out, however, to make sense of new and strange phenomena, one must be prepared to play with ideas. And I use the word "play" advisedly: dignified people, without a whimsical streak, almost never offer fresh insights, in economics or anywhere else. Suppose I tell you that "Japan is suffering from fundamental maladjustment, because its state-mediated growth model leads to structural rigidity." Well, guess what: I haven't said anything at all; at best I have conveyed a sense that the problems are very difficult, and there are no easy answers—a sense that may well be completely wrong. Suppose, on the other hand, that I illustrate Japan's problems with the entertaining tale of the ups and downs of a baby-sitting co-op (which will, in fact, make several appearances in this book). Maybe it sounds silly, maybe the levity will even offend your sensitivities, but the whimsicality has a purpose: it jolts the mind into a different channel, suggesting in this case that there may indeed be a surprisingly easy way out of at least part of Japan's problem. So don't expect a solemn, dignified book: the objectives here are as serious as can be, but the writing will be as silly as the subject demands.

And with that, let us begin our journey, starting with the world as it appeared to be, only two years ago.

The Return of

Depression

Economics

O N E

■

July 1, 1997

ONG Kong's elite may have been sleeping off the festivities of the previous night; but there was no break for the construction crews working frantically on Hong Kong's grandiose new convention center, trying to finish it in time to accommodate the annual joint meeting of the International Monetary Fund and the World Bank. Hosting this meeting—a pompous affair that attracts thousands of well-heeled camp followers, from industrialists to investment analysts—was a proud moment for Hong Kong: it symbolized the economic success not only of the city itself but of China and indeed of Asia as a whole.

Overlooking the construction site was a sleek modern tower, the New World Harbor Hotel. Inevitably, some of its guests rechristened it the New World *Order* Hotel. How could they resist?

The speechwriter who had George Bush proclaim that New World Order, oblivious to the Hitlerian echoes, may have had a tin ear. Yet he did have a point: truly, the world of the 1990s was one that would hardly have seemed possible even a few years earlier. Consider, for example, what happened (or more precisely what *didn't* happen) in the first few minutes of that July day, when Hong Kong itself was finally returned to Chinese rule—as a "Special Autonomous Region," to be sure, yet nonetheless finally and irrevocably a part of the People's Republic. Was anyone concerned? Well, some people worried that the handover would eventually lead to an erosion of civil liberties in the city-state; but nobody worried that Beijing was about to impose socialism. On the contrary, while China might have occupied Hong Kong, ideologically Hong Kong had conquered China: a government that had once sent anyone suspected of bourgeois attitudes to hard labor in the countryside was now dedicated to Deng Xiaoping's creed that "to grow rich is glorious." And as a result, the transfer of power that day seemed to proclaim the triumph not of socialism but of capitalism—a system so successful, so dominant, that even the People's Army posed no threat to business as usual.

Nobody knew it at the time, but the summer of 1997 would turn out to have been a sort of high-water mark for the New World Order. Capitalism's successes were not as solid as they seemed; over the next eighteen months a series of financial disasters would put much of the world's prosperity at risk and raise again some old questions about a system that relies on the invisible hand to direct private interest to public ends. But let us forget for a while about the hard lessons soon to be learned, and look at the world as it seemed to be on that day in July.

Capitalism Triumphant

This is a book about economics; but economics inevitably takes place in a political context, and one cannot understand the world as it appeared in that golden summer without considering the fundamental political fact of the 1990s: the collapse of socialism, not merely as a ruling ideology, but as an idea with the power to move men's minds.

That collapse began, rather oddly, in China. It is still mind-boggling to realize that Deng Xiaoping launched his nation on what turned out to be the road to capitalism in 1978, only three years after the Communist victory in Vietnam, only two years after the internal defeat of radical Maoists who wanted to resume the Cultural Revolution. Probably Deng did not fully realize how far that road would lead; certainly it took the rest of the world a long time to grasp that a billion people had quietly abandoned Marxism. In fact, as late as the early 1990s China's transformation had failed fully to register with the chattering classes; in the best-sellers of the time, the world economy was an arena for "head to head" struggle between Europe, America, and Japan—China was thought of, if at all, as a subsidiary player, perhaps part of an emerging yen bloc.

Nonetheless, everyone realized that something had changed, and that "something" was the collapse of the Soviet Union.

Nobody really understands what happened to the Soviet regime. With the benefit of hindsight we now think of the whole structure as a sort of ramshackle affair, doomed to eventual failure. Yet this was a regime that had maintained its grip through civil war and famine, that had been able against terrible odds to defeat Germany's original New Order, that was able to mobilize the scientific and industrial resources to contest America's nuclear superiority. How it could have ended so suddenly, not with a bang but with a whimper, should be regarded as one of the great puzzles of political economy. Maybe it was simply a matter of time—it seems that revolutionary fervor, above all the willingness to murder your opponents in the name of the greater good, cannot last more than a couple of generations. Or maybe the regime was gradually undermined by the stubborn refusal of capitalism to display the proper degree of decadence: I have a private theory, based on no evidence whatsoever, that the rise of Asia subtly but deeply demoralized the Soviet regime, by making its claim to have history on its side ever less plausible. A nasty, unwinnable war in Afghanistan certainly helped the process along, as did the evident inability of Soviet industry to match Ronald Reagan's arms buildup. But never mind: whatever the reasons, in 1989 the

Soviet empire in Eastern Europe suddenly unraveled, and in 1991 so did the Soviet Union itself.

The effects of that unraveling were felt around the world, in ways obvious and subtle. And all of the effects were favorable to the political and ideological dominance of capitalism.

First of all, of course, several hundred million people who had lived under Marxist regimes suddenly became citizens of states prepared to give markets a chance. Somewhat surprisingly, however, this has in some ways turned out to be the least important consequence of the Soviet collapse. Contrary to what most people expected, the "transition economies" of Eastern Europe did not quickly become a major force in the world market, or a favored destination for foreign investment. On the contrary, for the most part they had a very hard time making the transition: East Germany, for example, has become Germany's equivalent of Italy's Mezzogiorno, a permanently depressed region that is a continual source of social and fiscal concern. Only now, a decade after the fall of Communism, are a few countries—Poland, Estonia, the Czech Republic—starting to look like success stories. And Russia itself has not only failed to make a convincing transition to the market; by borrowing substantial sums, in effect with its decaying nuclear arsenal as collateral, it has managed to turn itself into a surprisingly powerful source of financial instability for the rest of the world. But let's reserve that story for Chapter 7.

Another direct effect of the collapse of the Soviet regime was that other governments that had relied on its largesse were now on their own. Since some of these states had been idealized and idolized by opponents of capitalism, their sudden poverty—and the corresponding revelation of their previous dependency— helped to undermine the legitimacy of all such movements. When Cuba seemed a heroic nation, standing alone with clenched fist confronting the United States, it was an attractive symbol for revolutionaries across Latin America—far more attractive, of course, than the gray bureaucrats of Moscow. The shabbiness of post-Soviet Cuba is not only disillusioning in itself; it makes painfully clear that the heroic stance of the past was possible only because of huge subsidies from those very bureaucrats. Similarly, until the 1990s North Korea's government, for all its ghastliness, held a certain mystique for radicals, particularly among South Korean students. With its population literally starving because it no longer receives Soviet aid, the thrill is gone.

Yet another more or less direct effect of Soviet collapse was the disappearance of the many radical movements that, whatever their claims to represent a purer revolutionary spirit, were in fact able to operate only because Moscow provided the weapons, the training camps, and the money. Europeans like to point out that the radical terrorists of the seventies and eighties—Baader-Meinhof in Germany, the Red Army Brigades in Italy—all claimed to be true Marxists, unconnected with the corrupt old Communists in Russia. Yet we now know that they were deeply dependent on Soviet-bloc aid, and as soon as that aid vanished, so did the movements.

Most of all, the humiliating failure of the Soviet Union destroyed the socialist dream. For a century and a half the idea of socialism—from each according to his abilities, to each according to his needs—served as an intellectual focal point for those who disliked the hand the market dealt them. Nationalist leaders invoked socialist ideals as they blocked foreign investment or repudiated foreign debts; labor unions used the rhetoric of socialism as they demanded higher wages; even businessmen appealed to vaguely socialist principles when demanding tariffs or subsidies. And those governments that nonetheless embraced more or less free markets did so cautiously, a bit shamefacedly, because they always feared that too total a commitment to letting markets have their way would be seen as a brutal, inhumane, anti-*social* policy.

But who can now use the words of socialism with a straight face? As a member of the baby boomer generation, I can remember when the idea of revolution, of brave men pushing history forward, had a certain glamour. Now it is a sick joke: after all the purges and gulags, Russia is as backward and corrupt as ever; after all the Great Leaps and Cultural Revolutions,

China has decided that making money is the highest good. There are still radical leftists out there, who stubbornly claim that true socialism has not yet been tried; and there are still moderate leftists, who claim with more justification that one can reject Marxist-Leninism without necessarily becoming a disciple of Milton Friedman. But the truth is that the heart has gone out of the opposition to capitalism.

And that is the essence of the New World Order. For the first time since 1917, we live in a world in which property rights and free markets are viewed as fundamental principles, not grudging expedients; where the unpleasant aspects of a market system—inequality, unemployment, injustice—are accepted as facts of life. As in the Victorian era, capitalism is secure not only because of its successes—which, as we will see in a moment, have been very real—but because nobody has a plausible alternative.

This situation will not last forever. Surely there will be other ideologies, other dreams; and they will emerge sooner rather than later if the Great Recession persists and deepens. But in that glorious summer of 1997 capitalism, for the first time in eighty years, ruled the world unchallenged.

The Taming of the Business Cycle

The great enemies of capitalist stability have always been war and depression. What George Bush—who, to his misfortune, never had much interest in economics—really meant by the New World Order was not so much the triumph of capitalism as the supposed emergence, after the 1991 Gulf War, of an international system that would prevent future wars. Tell it to the Bosnians or the Rwandans. But the collapse of the Soviet Union did leave the United States with such an overwhelming monopoly of military power that it is hard to see how a *major* war could erupt in the foreseeable future.

What about depression? The Great Depression came pretty close to destroying both capitalism and democracy, and led more or less directly to war. It was followed, however, by a generation of sustained growth in the industrial world, during which recessions were short and mild, recoveries strong and sustained. By the late 1960s the United States had gone so long without a recession that economists were holding conferences with titles like "Is the Business Cycle Obsolete?"

The question was premature: the 1970s were the decade of "stagflation," economic slump and inflation combined; and as I mentioned in the introduction, the two energy crises of 1973 and 1979 were followed by the worst recessions since the 1930s. But by the 1990s the question was being asked again; as unemployment fell year after year, as stock prices seemed to rise without limit, more and more pundits declared that we had indeed entered a new age of economic stability. In that golden July of 1997 *Foreign Affairs* published an article entitled "The End of the Business Cycle?" whose conclusion basically dropped the question mark. To much greater fanfare, in the same month *Wired* published Peter Schwartz and Peter Leyden's enthusiastic "The Long Boom: A History of the Future." Neither article, if read closely, claimed that the future would be free from occasional setbacks; but both did claim that the days of really severe recessions, let alone worldwide depressions, were behind us.

How would you make up your mind about something like that, other than by noticing that the economy has not had a major recession lately? To answer that question we need to make a digression into theory and ask ourselves what the business cycle is all about in the first place. In particular, why do market economies experience recessions?

Whatever you do, don't say that the answer is obvious—that recessions occur because of X, where X is the prejudice of your choice. The truth is that if you think about it—especially if you understand and generally believe in the idea that markets usually manage to match supply and demand—a recession is a very peculiar thing indeed. For during an economic slump, especially a severe one, supply seems to be everywhere and demand nowhere. There are willing workers but not enough jobs, perfectly good factories but not enough orders, open shops but not enough customers. It's easy enough to see how there can be a shortfall of demand for *some* goods: if manufacturers produce a lot of Beanie Babies, but it turns out that consumers want Furbys instead, some of those Beanie Babies may go unsold. But how can there be too little demand for goods in general? Don't people have to spend their money on *something*?

Part of the problem people have in talking sensibly about recessions is that it is hard to picture what is going on during a slump, to reduce it to a human scale. But I have a favorite story that I like to use, both to explain what recessions are all about and as an "intuition pump" for my own thought. (Readers of my earlier books have heard this one before.) It is a true story, although in Chapter 4 I will use an imaginary elaboration to try to make sense of Japan's malaise.

The story is told in an article by Joan and Richard Sweeney, published in 1978 under the title "Monetary Theory and the Great Capitol Hill Baby-sitting Co-op Crisis." Don't recoil at the title: this is serious.

During the 1970s the Sweeneys were members of, surprise, a baby-sitting cooperative: an association of young couples, in this case mainly people with congressional jobs, who were willing to baby-sit each other's children. This particular co-op was unusually large, about 150 couples, which meant that there were plenty of potential baby-sitters, but also that managing the organization—especially making sure that each couple did its fair share—was not a trivial matter.

Like many such institutions (and other barter schemes), the Capitol Hill co-op dealt with the problem by issuing scrip: coupons entitling the bearer to one hour of baby-sitting. When babies were sat, the baby-sitters would receive the appropriate number of coupons from the baby-sittees. This system was, by construction, shirkproof: it automatically ensured that over time each couple would provide exactly as many hours of baby-sitting as it received.

But it was not quite that simple. It turns out that such a system requires a fair amount of scrip in circulation. Couples with several free evenings in a row, and no immediate plans to go out, would try to accumulate reserves for the future; this accumulation would be matched by the running down of other couples' reserves, but over time each couple would on the average probably want to hold enough coupons to go out several times between bouts of baby-sitting. The issuance of coupons in the Capitol Hill co-op was a complicated affair: couples received coupons on joining, were supposed to repay them on leaving, but also paid dues in baby-sitting coupons that were used to pay officers, and so on. The details aren't important; the point is that there came a time when relatively few coupons were in circulation—too few, in fact, to meet the co-op's needs.

The result was peculiar. Couples who felt their reserves of coupons to be insufficient were anxious to baby-sit and reluctant to go out. But one couple's decision to go out was another's opportunity to baby-sit; so opportunities to baby-sit became hard to find, making couples even more reluctant to use their reserves except on special occasions, which made baby-sitting opportunities even scarcer . . .

In short, the co-op went into a recession.

Okay, time out. How do you react to being told this story?

If you are baffled—wasn't this supposed to be a book about the world economic crisis, not about child care?—you have missed the point. The only way to make sense of any complex system, be it global weather or the global economy, is to work with models—simplified representations of that system which you hope help you understand how it works. Sometimes models consist of systems of equations, sometimes of computer programs (like the simulations that give you your daily weather forecast); but sometimes they are like the model airplanes that designers test in wind tunnels, small-scale versions of the real thing that are more accessible to observation and experiment. The Capitol Hill Baby-sitting Co-op was a miniature economy; it was indeed just about the smallest economy capable of having a recession. But what it experienced *was* a real recession, just as the lift generated by a model airplane's wings is real lift; and just as the behavior of that model can give designers valuable insights into how a jumbo jet will perform, the ups and downs of the co-op can give us crucial insights into why full-scale economies succeed or fail.

If you are not so much puzzled as offended—we're supposed to be discussing important issues here, and instead you are being told cute little parables about Washington yuppies— shame on you. Remember what I said in the introduction: whimsicality, a willingness to play with ideas, is not merely entertaining but essential in times like these. Never trust an aircraft designer who refuses to play with model airplanes, and never trust an economic pundit who refuses to play with model economies.

As it happens, the tale of the baby-sitting co-op will turn out to be a powerful tool for understanding the not at all whimsical problems of real-world economies. The theoretical models economists use, mainly mathematical constructs, often sound far more complicated than this; but usually their lessons can be translated into simple parables like that of the Capitol Hill co-op (and if they can't, often this is a sign that something is wrong with the model). I will end up returning to the baby-sitting story several times in this book, in a variety of contexts. For now, however, let's consider two crucial implications of the story: one about how recessions can happen, the other about how to deal with them.

First, why did the baby-sitting co-op get into a recession? It was *not* because the members of the co-op were doing a bad job of baby-sitting: maybe they were, maybe they weren't, but anyway that is a separate issue. It wasn't because the co-op suffered from "Capitol Hill values," or engaged in "crony baby-sittingism," or had failed to adjust to changing baby-sitting technology as well as its competitors. The problem was not with the co-op's ability to produce, but simply a lack of "effective demand": too little spending on real goods (baby-sitting time), because people were trying to accumulate cash (baby-sitting coupons) instead. The lesson for the real world is that your vulnerability to the business cycle may have little or nothing to do with your more fundamental economic strengths and weaknesses: bad things can happen to good economies.

Second, in that case, what was the solution? The Sweeneys report that in the case of the Capitol Hill co-op it was quite dif-

ficult to convince the governing board, which consisted mainly of lawyers, that the problem was essentially technical, with an
easy fix. The co-op's officers at first treated it as what an economist would call a "structural" problem, requiring direct action:
a rule was passed *requiring* each couple to go out at least twice
a month. Eventually, however, the economists prevailed, and
the supply of coupons was increased. The results were magical:
with larger reserves of coupons couples became more willing to
go out, making opportunities to baby-sit more plentiful, making
couples even more willing to go out, and so on. The co-op's
GBP—gross baby-sitting product, measured in units of babies
sat—soared. Again, this was not because the couples had
become better baby-sitters, or that the co-op had gone through
any sort of fundamental reform process; it was simply because
the monetary screwup had been rectified. Recessions, in other
words, can be fought simply by printing money—and can
sometimes (usually) be cured with surprising ease.

And with that let us return to the business cycle in the full-
scale world.

The economy of even a small nation is, of course, far more
complex than that of a baby-sitting co-op. Among other things,
people in the larger world spend money not only for their current pleasure but to invest for the future (imagine hiring co-op
members not to watch your babies but to build a new playpen).
And in the big world there is also a capital market, in which
those with spare cash can lend it at interest to those who need it
now. But the fundamentals are the same: a recession is normally a matter of the public as a whole trying to accumulate cash
(or, what is the same thing, trying to save more than it invests)
and can normally be cured simply by issuing more coupons.

The coupon issuers of the modern world are known as central banks: the Federal Reserve, the Bank of England, the Bank
of Japan, and so on. And it is their job to keep the economy on
an even keel by adding or subtracting cash as needed.

But if it's that easy, why do we ever experience economic
slumps? Why don't the central banks always print enough
money to keep us at full employment?

Before World War II, the answer seems fairly straightforward: policy was ineffective because policymakers didn't know what they were doing. Nowadays practically the whole spectrum of economists, from Milton Friedman leftward, agrees that the Great Depression was brought on by a collapse of effective demand and that the Federal Reserve should have fought the slump with large injections of money. But at the time this was by no means the conventional wisdom. Indeed, many prominent economists subscribed to a sort of moralistic fatalism, which viewed the Depression as an inevitable consequence of the economy's earlier excesses, and indeed as a healthy process: recovery, declared Joseph Schumpeter, "is sound only if it [comes] of itself. For any revival which is merely due to artificial stimulus leaves part of the work of depressions undone and adds, to an undigested remnant of maladjustment, new maladjustment of its own which has to be liquidated in turn, thus threatening business with another [worse] crisis ahead."

Such fatalism vanished after the war, and for a generation most countries did try actively to control the business cycle, with considerable success; recessions were mild, and jobs were usually plentiful. By the late 1960s many started to believe that the business cycle was no longer a major problem; even Richard Nixon promised to "fine-tune" the economy.

This was hubris; and the tragic flaw of full-employment policies became apparent in the 1970s. If the central bank is overoptimistic about how many jobs can be created, if it puts too much money into circulation, the result is inflation; and once that inflation has become deeply embedded in the public's expectations, it can be wrung out of the system only through a period of temporarily high unemployment. Add in some external shock that suddenly increases prices—such as a doubling of the price of oil—and you have a recipe for nasty, if not Depression-sized, economic slumps.

But by the middle of the 1980s inflation had fallen back to tolerable levels, oil was in abundant supply, and central bankers finally seemed to be getting the hang of economic management. Indeed, the bad things that happened seemed, if anything, to reinforce the sense that we had finally figured this thing out. In 1987, for example, the U.S. stock market crashed—with a one-day fall that was as bad as the first day's fall of the 1929 crash. But the Federal Reserve pumped cash into the system, the real economy didn't even slow down, and the Dow soon recovered. At the end of the 1980s central bankers, worried about a small rise in inflation, missed the signs of a developing recession and got behind the curve in fighting it; but while that recession cost George Bush his job, eventually it responded to the usual medicine, and the United States entered into another period of sustained expansion. By the summer of 1997 it did indeed seem that the business cycle, if it had not been eliminated, had at least been decisively tamed.

Much of the credit for that taming went to the money managers: never in history has a central banker enjoyed quite the mystique of Alan Greenspan. But there was also a sense that the underlying structure of the economy had changed in ways that made continuing prosperity more likely.

The Wired *Age*

You don't have to like the magazine *Wired*, or even read it (those clashing colors and typefaces!), to regard it as a sort of quintessential publication of the nineties, with its fascination with technology, its breathless style—things! are changing! so fast! that we have to use lots!! of exclamation points!!!!—and, of course, its libertarian politics.

Why did these attributes form a natural, if often unreadable, package? Let's take a look at the information technology revolution and ask what it meant—not only to the reality of capitalism but to the way it was perceived.

In a strict technological sense you could say that the modern information age began when Intel introduced the microprocessor—the guts of a computer on a single chip—back in 1971. By the early 1980s products that put this technology to highly visible use—fax machines, video games, and personal computers—were becoming widespread. But at the time it didn't feel like a revolution. Most people assumed that the information industries would continue to be dominated by big, bureaucratic companies like IBM—or that all of the new technologies would eventually go the way of the fax machine, the VCR, and the video game: invented by innovative Americans, but converted into a paying product only by faceless Japanese manufacturers.

By the nineties, however, it was clear that the information industries would dramatically change the look and feel of our economy.

It is still possible to be skeptical about how large the actual economic benefits of information technology really are. Certainly the payoff in terms of measured productivity has been rather elusive; equally certainly that measurement understates the true gains; but whether the understatement is any worse than it was for previous technologies is anybody's guess. What cannot be denied is that the new technologies have had a more *visible* impact on how we work than anything in the previous twenty or thirty years. The typical modern American worker, after all, now sits in an office; and from 1900 until the 1980s the basic appearance of and working of a business office—typewriters and file cabinets, memos and meetings—was pretty much static. (Yes, the Xerox machine did do away with carbon paper.) Then, over a fairly short time, the whole thing changed: networked PCs on every desk, e-mail and the Internet, videoconferencing and telecommuting. This was qualitative, unmistakable change, which created a sense of major progress in a way that mere quantitative improvements could not. And that sense of progress helped bring with it a new sense of optimism about capitalism.

Moreover, the new industries brought back what we might call the romance of capitalism: the idea of the heroic entrepreneur who builds a better mousetrap, and in so doing becomes deservedly wealthy. Ever since the days of Henry Ford, that heroic figure had come to seem ever more mythical, as the economy became increasingly dominated by giant corporations, run not by romantic innovators but by bureaucrats who might just as well have been government officials. In 1968 John Kenneth Galbraith wrote,"With the rise of the modern corporation, the emergence of the organization required by modern technology and planning and the divorce of the owner of capital from control of the enterprise, the entrepreneur no longer exists as an individual person in the mature industrial enterprise." And who could be enthusiastic about capitalism that seemed more or less like socialism without the justice?

The information industries, however, shook up the industrial order. As in the nineteenth century, the economic story became one of remarkable individuals: of men (and, at least occasionally, women) who had a better idea, developed it in their garage or on their kitchen table, and struck it rich. Business magazines actually became interesting to read; and business success came to seem admirable, in a way that it hadn't for more than a century.

And this provided fertile ground for free-market ideas, even the libertarianism of *Wired*. Thirty years ago, defenders of the free market, of the virtues of untrammeled entrepreneurship, had an image problem: when they said "private enterprise," most people thought of General Motors; when they said "businessman," most people thought of the man in the gray flannel suit. In the 1990s the old idea that wealth is the product of virtue, or at least of creativity, made a comeback.

But what really made that summer of 1997 such a time of optimism was the remarkable spread of prosperity—not merely to the advanced nations (where, indeed, the benefits were not as widely spread as one might have wished) but to many countries that not long ago had been written off as economically hopeless.

The Fruits of Globalization

The term "Third World" was originally intended as a badge of pride: Jawaharlal Nehru coined it to refer to those countries that maintained their independence, allying themselves neither with the West nor with the Soviet Union. But soon enough the political intention was overwhelmed by the economic reality: "Third World" came to mean backward, poor, less developed. And the term came to carry a connotation not of righteous demand but of hopelessness.

What changed all of that was globalization: the transfer of technology and capital from high-wage to low-wage countries, and the resulting growth of labor-intensive Third World exports.

It is a bit hard to remember what the world looked like before globalization; so let's try to turn the clock back for a moment, to the Third World as it was less than a generation ago (and still is, in many countries). In those days, although the rapid economic growth of a handful of small East Asian nations had started to attract attention, developing countries like the Philippines, or Indonesia, or Bangladesh were still mainly what they had always been: exporters of raw materials, importers of manufactures. Small, inefficient manufacturing sectors served their domestic markets, sheltered behind import quotas, but these sectors generated few jobs. Meanwhile, population pressure pushed desperate peasants into cultivating ever more marginal land, or into seeking a livelihood in any way possible, such as homesteading on the mountains of garbage found near many Third World cities.

Given this lack of other opportunities, you could hire workers in Djakarta or Manila for a pittance. But in the mid-1970s cheap labor was not enough to allow a developing country to compete in world markets for manufactured goods. The entrenched advantages of advanced nations—their infrastructure and technical know-how, the vastly larger size of their markets and their proximity to suppliers of key components, their political stability and the subtle but crucial social adaptations that are necessary to operate an efficient economy—seemed to outweigh even a ten- or twentyfold disparity in wage rates. Even radicals seemed to despair of reversing those entrenched advantages: in the 1970s demands for a New International Economic Order were centered on attempts to increase the price of raw materials, rather than to bring Third World countries into the modern industrial world.

And then something changed. Some combination of factors that we still don't fully understand—lower tariff barriers, improved telecommunications, the advent of cheap air transport—reduced the disadvantages of producing in developing countries. Other things being the same, it is still better to produce in the First World—stories of firms that moved production to Mexico or East Asia, then decided to move back after experiencing the disadvantages of the Third World environment at first hand are actually quite common—but there were now a substantial number of industries in which low wages gave developing countries enough of a competitive advantage to break into world markets. And so countries that previously made a living selling jute or coffee started producing shirts and sneakers instead.

Workers in those shirt and sneaker factories are, inevitably, paid very little and expected to endure terrible working conditions. I say inevitably because their employers are not in business for their (or their workers') health; they will of course try to pay as little as possible, and that minimum is determined by the other opportunities available to workers. And in many cases these are still extremely poor countries.

Yet in those countries where the new export industries took root, the twenty or so years leading up to that golden summer of 1997 were a time of unmistakable improvement in the lives of ordinary people. Partly this is because a growing industry must offer its workers a somewhat higher wage than they could get elsewhere just in order to get them to move. More important, however, the growth of manufacturing, and of the penumbra of other jobs that the new export sector created, had a ripple effect throughout the economy. The pressure on the land became less intense, so rural wages rose; the pool of unemployed urban dwellers always anxious for work shrank, so factories started to compete with one another for workers, and urban wages also began to rise. In countries where the process had gone on long enough—say, in South Korea or Taiwan—average wages actually started to approach what an American teenager could earn at McDonalds. (In 1975 the average hourly wage in South Korea was only 5 percent of that in the United States; by 1996 it had risen to 46 percent.)

The benefits of export-led economic growth to the mass of people in the newly industrializing economies were not a matter of conjecture. A place like Indonesia is still so poor that progress can be measured in terms of how much the average person gets to eat; between 1968 and 1990 per capita intake rose from 2,000 to 2,700 calories a day, and life expectancy rose from forty-six years to sixty-three. Similar improvements could be seen throughout the Pacific Rim, and even in places like Bangladesh. These improvements did not take place because well-meaning people in the West did anything to help—foreign aid, never large, shrank in the 1990s to virtually nothing. Nor was it the result of the benign policies of national governments, which, as we were soon to be forcefully reminded, were as callous and corrupt as ever. It was the indirect and unintended result of the actions of soulless multinational corporations and rapacious local entrepreneurs, whose only concern was to take advantage of the profit opportunities offered by cheap labor. It was not an edifying spectacle; but no matter how base the motives of those involved, the result was to move hundreds of millions of people from abject poverty to something that was in some cases still awful but nonetheless significantly better.

And once again, capitalism could with considerable justification claim the credit. Socialists had long promised development; there was a time when the Third World looked to Stalin's five-year plans as the very image of how a backward nation should push itself into the twentieth century. And even after the Soviet Union had lost its aura of progressiveness, many intellectuals believed that only by cutting themselves off from competition with more advanced economies could poor nations hope to break out of their trap. By 1997, however, there were role models showing that rapid development was possible after all—and it had been accomplished not through proud socialist isolation but precisely by becoming as integrated as possible with global capitalism.

Skeptics and Critics

Not everyone was happy with the state of the world economy in the summer of 1997. While the United States was experiencing remarkable prosperity, other advanced economies were more troubled. Japan had never recovered from the bursting of its "bubble economy" at the beginning of the decade, and Europe was still suffering from "Eurosclerosis," the persistence of high unemployment rates, especially among the young, even during economic recoveries.

Nor did everyone in the United States share in the general prosperity. The forces of technological change and globalization had made it easier than ever before to grow truly rich, and raised the demand for highly skilled workers in general; but they had reduced the demand for the less skilled. Inequality of both wealth and income had increased to levels not seen since Great Gatsby days, and by official measures real wages had actually declined for many workers. Even if the numbers were taken with a grain of salt, it was pretty clear that the American economy's progress had left at least 20 or 30 million people at the bottom of the distribution slipping backward.

Some people found other things to be outraged about. The low wages and poor working conditions in those Third World export industries were a frequent source of moralizing—after all, by First World standards those workers were certainly miserable, and these critics had little patience with the argument that bad jobs at bad wages are better than no jobs at all. More justifiably, humanitarians pointed out that large parts of the world were completely untouched by the benefits of globalization: Africa, in particular, was still a continent of ever-deepening poverty, spreading disease, and brutal conflict.

And as always, there were doomsayers. It became particularly fashionable in 1996 or so to insist that global supply was outrunning global demand and that a day of reckoning was inevitable. But those who made this argument rarely had a good explanation of why growing incomes would not be spent, or why any shortfall in demand could not be easily handled, baby-sitting-co-op fashion, simply by increasing the money supply. (It turned out not to be that easy, after all, but for reasons the critics had never explained.) Anyway, there are always people predicting a new Great Depression; why should they have been taken more seriously in 1997 than at any other time?

Finally, even sensible people wondered whether the news was really good enough to justify the ever-rising U.S. stock market. In December 1996 Alan Greenspan famously warned the financial markets of the risks of "irrational exuberance"; stocks retreated briefly, then resumed their climb.

So it was not an entirely happy world on the day that Hong Kong reverted to China. But the prospects for the world economy in general, and for capitalism in particular, seemed better that day than they had been in living memory, better than anyone could have imagined a decade or two earlier.

The next day, July 2, Thailand devalued the baht, and the Asian financial crisis began.

A Short Course in Miracles:

Asia before the Crisis

I_T is always tempting to read history as if it were a mystery novel, in which all the earlier chapters contain clues that point the way to the thrilling conclusion, the moment when the astonishing truth is finally revealed. Yet to do so is often both to misrepresent the past and to be naive about the future. Consider, for example, the way America's Roaring Twenties looked to observers in the mid-1930s: few could avoid feeling that there must have been something bogus and unsound about the preceding decade's seeming prosperity—an unsoundness that became manifest in the end, when the economy plunged into depression. But the prosperity of the twenties was real, as were the industrial achievements that made it possible. To say that the excesses of those years made the subsequent crash inevitable may have seemed a straightforward reading of history, but was in fact a theoretical speculation— one that, as I will argue later in this book, is not only debatable but almost surely wrong. And anyway, the Depression was not the end of the story—indeed, there is *never* an end to the story. Sixty years on, it is the 1930s, not the 1920s, that look like the aberration; but then who is to say that this judgment, too, may not be premature?

Looking now at the humbled Asians—who used to ask how long it would be before they overtook the West, but now ask only how long it will take before they get back to where they were two years ago—we can all too easily project the recent disaster into the past. Weren't those economies really more show than substance, all facade with nothing behind it? Wasn't the "Asian miracle" really a figment of our imagination?

No. Asian growth was real, for the most part as impressive on closer examination as it appeared on the surface. The growth was not miraculous, if by a miracle one means something incomprehensible; nor was Asia's performance, for all its impressiveness, without some important—and surprising— flaws. But remember the lesson of the baby-sitting co-op: bad things can happen to good economies. Let us not assume that because something bad eventually happened, what preceded it was not truly, even astonishingly, good.

Tigers and Dragons

Economic growth, at least economic growth that raises living standards, is a modern invention. From the dawn of history to the eighteenth century, the world was essentially Malthusian: improvements in technology and capital investments were always overtaken by population growth; the number of people slowly increased, but their average standard of living did not. Louis XIV's subjects were probably no better nourished than the peasants of ancient Egypt. And billions of people—most of Africa, much of South Asia—still live right on the edge of subsistence.

Since the eighteenth century, however, one country after another has experienced what the Harvard economist Walt Whitman Rostow called the "takeoff into sustained growth." Rostow's once influential theory of that takeoff has long since fallen into disrepute, but the term itself remains compelling. Every once in a while, something happens to a previously stag-

nant economy: after decades or even centuries in which productivity and per capita income have gone nowhere, they begin
a steep climb, and the country is on its way to joining the modern world.

The first takeoff was, of course, the original Industrial Revolution in England, whose beginning is traditionally dated at
around 1790. Later other Western countries experienced their
own takeoffs: most notably, Germany (once a relatively poor
country) and the United States (which has always been relatively rich) industrialized at a pace that eventually allowed
them to overtake Britain's lead. In the late nineteenth century,
Japan became the first, and for a long time the only, non-West-
ern country to industrialize. There then followed a long pause:
from the late nineteenth century to the 1960s, the advanced
economies continued to grow, but no new members joined
their club. Indeed, it began to seem as if the division between
First World and Third World was a permanent one.

And then came the industrialization of Asia. First were the
original tigers: Hong Kong, Singapore, Taiwan, South Korea,
all of which began their economic ascent in the 1960s. Then
came the second wave: the poor but populous economies of
Southeast Asia. And finally there was the astonishing takeoff of
the great dragon itself, China.

To appreciate the magnitude of this achievement one must
realize that it broke through a long-standing historic barrier:
until Asian economies began to take off, economic development appeared to be a Western specialty, with only Japan—a
country arguably in a class of its own—to challenge that
monopoly. One must also realize just how many people were
involved: the "miracle" economies of Asia are home to a quarter of humanity. But what is really striking to an economist is
the sheer speed of the takeoff: never before have economies
risen so quickly.

Here are a few comparisons. From 1801 to 1851, as Britain
transformed itself from the largely rural nation of Jane Austen
to the urban-industrial nation of Charles Dickens, its per capita GDP grew at the hitherto unprecedented rate of 1.3 percent

per year. From 1870 to 1913, as the United States underwent a similar transition—and muscled aside Britain as the world's leading industrial power—per capita output rose 2.2 percent per annum. Japan was already an industrialized nation before World War II; so looking at its high-growth years after the war is cheating a bit. But the stunning speed with which it emerged from the ruin of war to become the world's second-largest economy—8 percent per capita growth from 1953 to 1973—was something new under the sun: no economy had ever grown that fast before, and few thought that any ever would again.

But then came the tigers and the dragons. In 1963 South Korea instituted an economic reform that, to everyone's surprise, began the transformation of a poverty-stricken nation, surviving largely on U.S. aid, into one of history's great success stories. Over the next thirty-four years, per capita income in Korea rose almost 7 percent per annum, a ninefold increase in little more than one generation. One way to put this in perspective is to notice that in 1963 South Korea was probably poorer than Britain had been in 1800—poorer, perhaps, than Britain had been since the seventeenth century. By 1997 the Koreans had reached more or less the per capita income of Britain in the early 1960s.

And finally, there is China, whose billion people quadrupled their incomes in less than two decades. Never in human history have so many people experienced so rapid an improvement in their material status.

Given this extraordinary achievement, what fault could anyone find with Asia's performance? Let us consider first the foolish caveats, then the more serious ones.

How Real Was the Growth?

How could one argue with the kind of success just described? The truth is that not many people tried. Still, there were some who argued before the crisis, and many more after, that Asia's success was not all that it seemed. Broadly, these arguments fell into three categories.

First, some people wondered whether the numbers were truly to be believed. Partly this was a question of simple honesty: in general, senior government officials like to hear good news, and those who depend on their favor—not only the employees of the statistical office but also the local administrators and businessmen whose reports provide the raw data with which the statistical office works—can easily be tempted to prettify the truth. In a well-run government, strong measures are taken to keep this sort of thing from happening: those who make policy are separated by a not-to-be-breached "Chinese wall" of secrecy and civil service regulations from those who provide data on the success or failure of that policy. But there is no Chinese wall in China—or, for that matter, in many other countries. So one could be forgiven for suspecting that things were not quite as good as the numbers implied. (When another wall, the one that divided Berlin, fell, economists learned just how badly the statistics of an authoritarian state can misrepresent the truth. According to its own figures, East Germany's per capita income was about 80 percent that of West Germany—higher, indeed, than that of some West German *Länder*. What was revealed on reunification was an economy that looked, well, Third World.)

More broadly, anyone who has seen how economic statistics are constructed knows that they are really a subgenre of science fiction. Real gross domestic product is, in principle, constructed by valuing everything the economy produces at the prices of some base year. But no statistical agency can really keep track of everything that is produced, or put a price on every product (indeed, this may be impossible even in principle, if the good in question—say, Viagra—wasn't available at any price in the base year). So actual estimates of economic growth are based on a good deal of fudging: on "imputations" and approximations. This can be done well or badly; in the United States the men and women who prepare statistics are scrupulous and careful, doing the best job possible given their limited resources and the inherent difficulties of their task. Elsewhere the job is less well done. I personally once consulted for a government that each year published many charts and tables describing the growth of national income, but which at the time really collected only about a dozen actual statistics (among them agricultural production numbers supplied by the United States, thanks to satellite photos) and based the rest on fairly casual guesswork.

So one could be forgiven for suspecting that the numbers about Asian growth might well be a bit too good to be true. Some experts on China, in particular, believe that a more scrupulously collected and analyzed set of figures would show growth a couple of percentage points slower than the official statistics; and perhaps similar if smaller corrections would have been appropriate elsewhere in the region.

But no such adjustment will take away the fact of awesome economic progress. For one need not look only at official growth statistics. Asia's progress was visible to the naked eye: skyscrapers where once there were only huts, roads where once there were only tracks, cars where once there were only bicycles. Wages rose rapidly—not just in the official statistics but in the experience of private companies that had to attract workers. And of course somebody was obviously making enough money to buy all those consumer goods and fly on all those new passenger routes.

Asia's growth, then, was real. But was it solid? Or was it all based on borrowed money?

This is not an idle question. The idea of a country, or even a whole region, that for some reason becomes a favorite of investors, and as a result experiences a temporary boom that is not grounded in fundamental productive success, is by no means hypothetical. Mexico in the late 1970s, Mexico again in the early 1990s, Russia in 1995–98: all were places that experienced a feverish consumption boom driven by foreign investment for a few years, only to crash when those same foreign investors concluded that the real economy to justify their investments simply wasn't there. (More on all these stories in later chapters.) Was Asia just another case of gullible investors giving an economy too much credit?

The answer turns out to be easy: from the beginning of the Asian takeoff to the early 1990s, the region's growth was overwhelmingly financed on a pay-as-you-go basis, out of each country's own savings. Little money was borrowed; most of the capital that came from abroad took the form of "direct" foreign investment, that is, foreign companies building plants, usually to serve export markets. If there was a speculative fever—and there was—it came only late in the game and does not call into question the reality of the growth before then.

So could anything negative be said about Asian growth? Yes: but it takes a bit of explaining.

Inspiration versus Perspiration

Until the coming of the financial crisis, the only serious critique of Asian performance revolved around a mysterious-sounding concept: "total factor productivity." It was the one yardstick by which Asia did not excel, and hence the one indicator of possible future trouble that received wide discussion before, as opposed to after, disaster actually struck.

Usually when people talk about "productivity" they really mean "labor productivity"—the amount that a worker can produce within a specified period of time, such as an hour or a year. Over the long run, labor productivity and economic growth are virtually synonymous. American workers are roughly seven times as productive as they were a century ago; that is why real wages and average family income are also roughly seven times what they were in 1900. And Asian labor productivity has grown almost as impressively as everything else.

But how do nations raise their labor productivity, and have Asians done it the "right" way? That is where the controversy arose.

One way to make a worker more productive is to give him better equipment. A man with a bulldozer can dig more ditches in a year than a man equipped only with a shovel; an actuary with a computer can do more accounts than one who must add and subtract by hand. And investment, which creates the capital equipment with which workers are equipped, is surely a major force for economic growth.

But the facts suggest that capital accumulation cannot have been the *only* source of long-run growth. For one thing, in 1900 you simply couldn't have equipped a ditchdigger with a bulldozer, or an actuary with a computer: they did not exist. (Steam-driven earthmoving machines did exist—they were used to build the Panama Canal—but they were huge and clumsy, not suited for most ordinary jobs. And mechanical adding machines also existed, but—having used one during a summer job in 1970—I can assure you that they were not much better than paper and pencil.) So even if employers in 1900 had spent as much in inflation-adjusted dollars equipping their workers as their counterparts a century later, they would not have achieved the same results, because the technology wasn't there. Rising labor productivity, in other words, has not been simply a matter of giving labor more capital to work with; it has also been the result of improved technology. It is, in other words, the result of inspiration as well as perspiration.

We can also see the importance of technology to economic growth by looking at some more quantitative measures. One is to look not at the productivity of labor but at that of capital. Suppose you were to compare two otherwise equivalent groups of workers, one equipped with $10,000 worth of machinery per man, the other with $20,000. Surely the latter group would be more productive than the former; but almost equally surely it would not be twice as productive. Capital, like any resource, is subject to "diminishing returns": the more of it you use, the less you gain from each additional increment. But if workers equipped with twice as much capital produce less than twice as much output, then output per unit of capital—capital productivity—is lower for that second group than for the first.

What this means is that if simple accumulation of capital were the main force behind economic growth, we would expect to see declining capital productivity as the counterpart of rising labor productivity. But looking at the long-term history of Britain or the United States, one sees instead that capital and output per worker have grown roughly in tandem, with no sign of diminishing returns.

Can one go beyond this general statement to assess the relative importance of capital accumulation and technology in economic growth? Well, one way to think about it is to say that improved technology generally allows you to get more output from a given amount of inputs—a modern worker with $20,000 worth of equipment can produce a lot more than a 1900 counterpart could have. (In fact, economists actually *define* technological progress by its results in allowing more output from given inputs.) So one could imagine assessing technological progress by measuring the productivity not of labor but of *inputs in general*—some composite of capital and labor.

You might object that there is no such thing as "inputs in general"—you can't add capital and labor, just as you can't add apples and oranges. But the fact is that we *do* add apples and oranges whenever we use a number like "real GDP," which adds the output of all goods, valued at constant prices. So why not do the same for capital and labor, creating an index of total input? And that, subject to some technical qualifications, is what economists do when they calculate "total factor productivity" (aka TFP) for an industry or the economy as a whole. It is an indirect measure of technological progress, calculated as the residual—the difference between the rates of growth of an index of input and an index of output.

To measure something is not to explain it. Indeed, MIT's Robert Solow, one of the founders of the modern theory of economic growth, described total factor productivity as "the measure of our ignorance." It is therefore a source of embarrassment for economists that most of the interesting action in economic growth usually turns out to arise from changes in this mysterious residual. Solow found, in a pioneering 1958 paper, that some 80 percent of the rise in output per worker in the United States over the preceding half century was "explained" by increased TFP; another early researcher, Edward Denison, found that the differences in growth rates among industrial countries—the slow growth of Britain, the rapid growth of Japan—were also explained mainly by differences in the rate of TFP growth. And when the growth of labor productivity in the United States suddenly and dismayingly slowed after 1973, the culprit turned out to be, yet again, total factor productivity.

Naturally enough, some economists have rebelled against so unhelpful a result. Some argued that early measures of total factor productivity growth were exaggerated, because they failed to take account of the rising education levels of workers—of increases in "human capital." (Most modern estimates take this into account.) Others argued that capital investment was more crucial to economic growth than the standard calculations suggested, because new technology could be put to work only if it was "embodied" in new machines. In any case, the usual problem facing analysts of economic growth is what more to say when high rates of growth are due mainly to high rates of increase in output per unit of input.

But there have been a few cases in which high economic growth does *not* seem to be mainly explained by large increases in overall productivity. And such cases are interesting, because the absence of the usual correlation between high growth and rapid productivity increase at least suggests both that something troubling may be going on and that the economy might face some difficulties in the future.

The classic case of high output growth without much productivity growth was that of the Soviet Union in the 1950s and early 1960s, the era during which Nikita Khrushchev, boasting about his country's industrial achievements, declared to the West, "We will bury you." At that very moment, American researchers (funded mainly by the CIA, whether they knew it or not) were finding, to their surprise, that while the Soviet economy was indeed growing very fast at that point, it was doing so only because of massive mobilization of labor and huge rates of investment—that total factor productivity was growing slowly, if at all. This implied that the growth would have to slow down: even the Soviets would eventually run out of housewives and peasants to force into their factories, and while they could con-

tinue to invest a huge share of output, they could not continu-
ally *increase* that share.

The stagnation of TFP also raised questions about the effectiveness of Soviet economic management. After all, Moscow
was devoting large resources to science and technology—
remember, this was the age of Sputnik. Furthermore, as a still
relatively backward economy, the Soviet Union ought to have
been able to achieve high productivity growth by borrowing
and adapting Western technologies. The fact that this was not
happening at least suggested that despite the regime's success
in mobilizing resources, it was not using those resources very
efficiently—perhaps indicating some deeper weaknesses in the
economic system.

Sure enough, a few years after Khrushchev pounded the UN
podium with his shoe, Soviet economic growth slowed sharply.
Instead of overtaking the West, the Soviet bloc began to fall
behind. The catastrophic collapse, first of the Soviet economy,
then of the state itself, still lay far in the future; but the calculation of total factor productivity had provided the first early
warning of troubles to come.

The second major example of economies whose rapid economic growth was not associated with corresponding improvements in total factor productivity was, it turned out, the case of
emerging Asia.

Among the first to notice this surprising fact was Stanford
University's Lawrence Lau, a careful, reserved researcher who
had spent many years developing sophisticated techniques for
the estimation of total factor productivity. When he and a co-
author turned these techniques loose on Asian countries, they
were surprised to find hardly any productivity growth—a result
that attracted relatively little attention at first.

Asia's productivity performance got a more aggressive discussion from Boston University's Alwyn Young, who began with a
study entitled "A Tale of Two Cities," comparing the economic growth of Hong Kong and that of Singapore. What he found
there was that Singapore had mobilized far more resources

than Hong Kong, in particular through extremely high rates of investment, yet had grown no faster, suggesting that those resources had not been used very efficiently. This discovery led him to a broader study of Asian growth—a study that found that Singapore's story, of rapid growth achieved through massive growth in inputs rather than growth of efficiency, was actually typical of the Asian tigers. Measuring total factor productivity rather than growth, he declared, brings Asian performance down "from the heights of Olympus to the plains of Thessaly."

Young's and Lau's work received wide publicity in 1994, when I wrote a summary of that work and its implications for *Foreign Affairs*, in an article entitled "The Myth of Asia's Miracle." That article, which used the example of the Soviet Union as a motivating device, elicited reactions that ranged from rage to blind fury. Both Asians and their Western admirers were quick to attack both the motives and the results of the researchers, arguing in particular that Young's and Lau's results depended on dubious assumptions, that there were other reasonable interpretations of the same data.

But there weren't. Alwyn Young, anticipating just such critiques, titled his crucial paper "The Tyranny of Numbers," by which he meant, "You may not like what I'm saying here, buster, but there is just no way around it." The fact was that anyone who applied the standard, conventional methods of such analysis—the same methods that were routinely used to estimate productivity in other countries—arrived at the same result. Those who got different answers always turned out to have done something funny with the data; indeed, it was often hard not to suspect that they had worked at the problem in a deliberate effort to avoid reaching the Young-Lau conclusion.

A case in point was the World Bank's 1993 study *The East Asian Miracle*. Tucked away in one of the appendixes of that report was a straightforward, conventional calculation of "technical efficiency change"—the rate at which Asian developing countries were converging on the productivity of advanced countries. The numbers looked like this:

Hong Kong 2.0
Taiwan 0.8
Thailand 0.1
Korea –0.2
Indonesia –1.2
Malaysia –1.8
Singapore –3.5

In other words, according to the World Bank's own estimates most Asian economies *weren't* closing the productivity gap — the median economy, Korea's, was actually slipping slightly backward. But this result was, as I said, tucked away in an appendix. The headline result was an alternative calculation (based not on market data but on a highly questionable statistical technique that was further biased by the inclusion of many "Fourth World" countries in the sample) that did seem to show rapid productivity growth in Asia — a result far more in keeping with the report's enthusiastic title.

The debate over Asian productivity still rages. Other studies, notably a comprehensive study by Susan Collins and Barry Bosworth of the Brookings Institution, have confirmed the Young-Lau result. Some critics have raised again the old objections to TFP calculations, missing the point that these objections are designed to explain why such calculations will produce a false positive, not a false negative. Some recent work by Princeton's Chang Hsieh does offer a serious critique: for Singapore he finds a conflict between two alternative measures of productivity growth and suggests that the reason may be bad data: Singapore has been overstating its true investment, and hence understating its true productivity. But the basic point remains: Asia achieved remarkable rates of economic growth without correspondingly remarkable increases in productivity. Its growth was the product of resource mobilization rather than efficiency, of perspiration rather than inspiration.

Why did this matter? The growth was still real, as were the dramatic improvements in the human condition. Who cares if the process was different from, perhaps cruder than, the standard route?

As in the case of the Soviet Union, one answer was that, given the lack of rapid productivity growth, Asia was bound to run into diminishing returns. By 1997 Malaysia was investing more than 40 percent of GDP, twice its share in the 1970s; Singapore was investing half its income. These rates of investment surely could not be pushed much higher; and merely maintaining them would not be enough to sustain high growth. One key indicator of the productivity of investment is the so-called ICOR (that's short for "incremental capital-output ratio")—the number of investment dollars needed to produce one more dollar of real GDP; throughout Southeast Asia these ICORs were increasing, clear evidence of diminishing returns. Given rising ICORs, growth could be sustained only via an ever-increasing investment rate, and that just wasn't going to happen.

Also as in the case of the Soviet Union, the failure to achieve productivity growth raised questions about the effectiveness of economic management in general. Until the Young-Lau results were publicized, many people—both Asian and Western—had extolled the virtues of a supposed "Asian system" in which markets were given strategic direction by government officials, supposedly achieving results superior to that of naive laissez-faire. But such a system, if successful, would presumably lead not just to mobilization of lots of resources but to their efficient use—so why wasn't efficiency rising? Moreover, again like the Soviet Union, Asia was still technologically behind the West, and should have been in a position to achieve rapid productivity growth by borrowing and adapting existing technologies. Why didn't this show in the data?

The funny thing was that anecdotes of technology transfer were legion. Asian factories, telecommunications, and construction methods clearly were becoming more efficient thanks to the importation of Western technology. Yet somehow these gains were being dissipated; while it had been spectacularly successful in mobilizing resources, the "Asian system" did not seem to be particularly effective at using those resources.

That is, if there was any such thing as an "Asian system" in the first place.

Was There an Asian System?

I've never been able to find it, but I distinctly remember an old interview in which Singapore's strongman Lee Kuan Yew attributed the rapid growth of his region to "the inner dynamism of East Asian man." I've always liked that line, if only because of the irony: if ever there was a case of top-down development, of a nation that grew not because of individual initiative but because the man in charge had a vision and imposed it on his countrymen, it was Mr. Lee's Singapore.

One might further ask whether it even makes sense to talk about "East Asian man." The countries that make up the World Bank's group of "high-performance Asian economies," or HPAEs (I think that's pronounced "hippies"), include the Moslem nations of Indonesia and Malaysia, the Buddhist kingdom of Thailand, the ethnic Chinese city-states of Singapore and Hong Kong, and the utterly distinctive cultures of Korea and Japan. (Recent evidence suggests that the Japanese are in fact ethnic Koreans and that their language descended from a southern Korean dialect; but that was a long time ago, and anyway the Japanese will never admit it.)

Yet the fact remains that all of these countries have achieved extraordinary growth rates. They also share other characteristics: very high savings rates, and unusually good basic education and correspondingly high rates of literacy and numeracy. The rapid accumulation of physical and human capital that resulted from these common traits, in turn, is the main explanation of their rapid economic growth. Why do these countries, with their evident differences, have so much in common?

The short answer is that nobody really knows. Some people, notably the political theorist Samuel Huntington, have argued that the whole area shares a "Confucian" culture. This may sound peculiar when applied to Indonesia or Malaysia, but the (socially divisive) truth is that in Southeast Asia the business

THE RETURN OF DEPRESSION ECONOMICS

elite is predominantly ethnic Chinese. Max Weber famously argued that the "Protestant ethic" explained the economic rise of northwestern Europe; perhaps a "Confucian ethic" of high saving and respect for education is the common theme of Asia's economic success. And maybe that is what Mr. Lee meant by the dynamism of East Asian man. Well, as Robert Solow—the same economist who described total factor productivity as the "measure of our ignorance"—once pointed out, efforts to explain differences in economic growth rates typically end in a "blaze of amateur sociology." Which is not to say that such sociological speculations may not be right.

However, some observers thought they saw a different commonality in Asian growth: the adoption of an "Asian system," modeled on the success of Japan, which tossed aside naive Western notions of laissez-faire and free trade in favor of a regime in which governments actively promoted particular businesses, protecting them from foreign competition until they were ready to start exporting, subsidizing them with cheap credit, and in general using the state as an instrument of economic development. Probably the high point of this view came with James Fallows's 1994 book *Looking at the Sun: The Rise of the New East Asian Economic and Political System*, which argued that Western countries themselves had developed only through state intervention, but that now it was the Asians who were able to dispense with the ideology of free trade and pursue economic growth single-mindedly. "[I]nconvenience to consumers," declared Fallows in a summary article, "is less damaging in the long run than weakness of a nation's productive base. The fastest-growing modern economies, in East Asia, reflect this view. Like it or not, we live in the world that Asian success stories have shaped. We need to figure out how to compete in it."

Or as another commentator put it, responding angrily to the suggestion that Asian productivity growth had been unimpressive, Asian growth had been achieved through the "interlocking cooperation of free enterprise, government financial intervention, and a guidance-minded technocratic bureaucracy. . . . It is a trick . . . that the managers of developed Western economies have yet to learn."

And he had a point. Asian economies were characterized by a different sort of governance from that of the United States. Instead of the kind of adversarial, legalistic relationship we have evolved between government and business, the HPAEs enjoyed an uninhibited closeness between the business and government elites, a sort of cozy collaborative relationship. My critic was sure that this closeness worked in the interest of the economy as a whole—that it allowed business and government to cooperate to maximize national wealth. Soon that same coziness would acquire a new name: "crony capitalism." It would be accused, correctly, of fostering private gain at the economy's expense and, less convincingly, of being at the root of the crisis.

But at the time crisis was hardly on anybody's mind, at least for Asia. Crises happened only in other places.

T H R E E

■

Warning Ignored:

Latin America, 1995

IMAGINE playing word association—in which one person says a word or phrase, and the other is supposed to reply with the first thing that pops into his mind—with an experienced international banker, finance official, or economist. Until very recently, and perhaps even now, if you said "financial crisis," he would surely reply "Latin America."

For generations, Latin American countries were almost uniquely subject to currency crises, banking failures, bouts of hyperinflation, and all the other monetary ills known to modern man. Weak elected governments alternated with military strongmen, both trying to buy popular support with populist programs they could not afford. In the effort to finance these programs, governments resorted either to borrowing from careless foreign bankers, with the end result being balance-of-payments crisis and default, or to the printing press, with the end result being hyperinflation. To this day, when economists tell parables about the dangers of "macroeconomic populism," about the many ways in which money can go bad, the hypothetical currency is by convention named the "peso."

But by the late 1980s it seemed that Latin America had final-ly learned its lesson. Few Latins admired the brutality of Augus-to Pinochet; but the economic reforms he launched in Chile proved highly successful and were preserved intact when Chile finally returned to democracy in 1989. Chile's return to the Victorian virtues — to sound money and free markets — began to look increasingly attractive as the country's growth rate acceler-ated. Moreover, the old policies seemed finally to have reached the end of the road: the debt crisis that began in 1982 dragged on and on, and it became increasingly clear that only some rad-ical change in policy would get the region moving again.

And so Latin America reformed. State-owned companies were privatized, restrictions on imports lifted, budget deficits trimmed. Controlling inflation became a priority; in some cases, as we will see, countries adopted drastic measures to restore confidence in their currencies. And these efforts were quickly rewarded not only with greater efficiency but in the renewed confidence of foreign investors. Countries that had spent the 1980s as financial pariahs — as late as 1990, creditors who wanted out of Latin debt and sold their claims to less risk-averse investors received, on average, only thirty cents on the dollar — became darlings of the international markets, receiving inflows of money that dwarfed even the bank loans that got them into the original debt crisis. International media began to talk about the "new" Latin America, in particular about the "Mexican miracle." In September 1994 the annual World Competitiveness Report, prepared by the people who run the famous Davos conferences, featured a special message from the hero of the hour, the Mexican president, Carlos Salinas.

Three months later, Mexico plunged into its worst financial crisis yet. The so-called tequila crisis caused one of the worst recessions to hit an individual country since the 1930s; its reper-cussions spread across Latin America, coming perilously close to bringing down Argentina's banking system. In retrospect, that crisis should have been seen as an omen, a warning that the good opinion of the markets can be fickle, that today's good press does not insulate you from tomorrow's crisis of confidence.

But the warning was ignored. To understand why, we need to look at the strangely underemphasized story of Latin America's great crisis.

Mexico: Up from the 1980s

Nobody could describe Mexico's government as unsophisticated. The president's inner circle, the so-called Científicos, were well-educated young men who wanted Mexico to become a modern nation and believed that this required close integration with the world economy. Foreign investors were welcomed, their property rights assured. And, impressed with the progressive leadership, they came in large numbers, playing a crucial role in the country's modernization.

But that was a long time ago. Porfirio Díaz, who ruled Mexico from 1876 to 1911, was eventually overthrown by a popular uprising. And the stable government that emerged after a decade of civil war was populist, nationalist, suspicious of foreign investors in general and the United States in particular. Members of the wonderfully named Institutional Revolutionary Party, or PRI, wanted to modernize Mexico, but they wanted to do it their way: industries were developed by domestic companies to serve the domestic market, sheltered from more efficient foreigners by tariffs and import restrictions. Foreign money was acceptable, as long as it did not bring foreign control; the Mexican government was happy to let its companies borrow from U.S. banks, as long as the voting shares remained in local hands.

This inward-looking economic policy may have been inefficient; aside from the *maquiladoras*, export-oriented factories that were allowed to operate only in a narrow zone near the U.S. border, Mexico failed to take advantage of the rising tide of globalization. But once established, Mexico's development policy became deeply entrenched in the country's political and social system, defended by an iron triangle of industrial oligarchs (who received preferential access to credit and import licenses), politicians (who received largesse from the oligarchs), and labor unions (which represented a "labor aristocracy" of relatively well-paid workers in the sheltered industries). Until the 1970s, it must also be said, Mexico was careful not to over-reach financially; growth was disappointing, but there were no crises.

In the late 1970s, however, that traditional caution was thrown to the winds. The economy entered a feverish boom, fed by new oil discoveries, high prices for that oil, and large loans from foreign banks.

Few people saw the warning signs. There were scattered press stories suggesting some emerging financial problems, but the general view was that Mexico (and Latin America in general) posed few financial risks. This complacency can be quantified: as late as July 1982 the yield on Mexican bonds was slightly *less* than that on those of presumably safe borrowers like the World Bank, indicating that investors regarded the risk that Mexico would fail to pay on time as negligible.

In the middle of the next month, however, a delegation of Mexican officials flew to Washington to inform the U.S. treasury secretary that they were out of money and that Mexico could no longer honor its debts. Within a few months the crisis had spread through most of Latin America and beyond, as banks stopped lending and began demanding repayment. Through frantic efforts—emergency loans from the U.S. government and international agencies like the Bank for International Settlements, "rescheduling" of loan repayments, and what was politely known as "concerted lending" (in which banks were more or less coerced into lending countries the money they needed to pay interest on outstanding loans)—most countries managed to avoid an outright default. The price of this narrow avoidance of financial catastrophe, however, was a severe recession, followed by a slow and often sputtering recovery. By 1986 real income per capita was 10 percent lower than it had been in 1981; real wages, eroded by an average inflation rate of more than 70 percent over the preceding four years, were 30 percent below their pre-crisis level.

Enter the reformers. Over the course of the 1970s a "new

class" had become increasingly influential within Mexico's ruling party and government. Well-educated, often with graduate
degrees from Harvard or MIT, fluent in English and interna-
tionalist in outlook, they were Mexican enough to navigate the
PRI's boss-and-patronage political waters, but Americanized
enough to believe that things should be different. The economic crisis left the old guard, the "dinosaurs," at a loss for
answers; the "technopols," who could explain how free-market
reforms had worked in Chile, how export-oriented growth had
worked in Korea, how inflation stabilization had been achieved
in Israel, found themselves the men of the hour. And by the
mid-1980s many Latin American economists had abandoned
the old statist views of the fifties and sixties in favor of what
came to be called the Washington Consensus: growth could
best be achieved via sound budgets, low inflation, deregulated
markets, and free trade.

In 1985 President Miguel de la Madrid began to put this
doctrine into effect, most dramatically through a radical freeing
up of Mexico's trade: tariffs were slashed, and the range of
imports requiring government licenses drastically reduced. The
government began selling off some of the enterprises it owned,
and loosened the strict rules governing foreign ownership. And
perhaps most remarkable of all, de la Madrid designated as his
successor not one of the usual PRI bosses but a champion of
the new reformers: Planning and Budget Secretary Carlos Salinas de Gortari, himself possessed of a degree from Harvard's
Kennedy School of Government, and surrounded by a staff of
highly regarded economists trained mainly at MIT.

I use the phrase "designated as his successor" advisedly. Mexico's political system from 1920 to 1990 was truly unique. On
paper it was a representative democracy; in recent years that
piece of fiction has, amazingly, started to become reality. But in
1988, the year Salinas was elected, Mexican democracy was
really a sort of souped-up version of traditional Chicago politics: a one-party system in which votes were bought through
patronage, and any shortfall was made up through creative vote
counting. The remarkable thing about this system, however,

was that the president himself, while very nearly an absolute monarch during his six-year term, could not seek a second term; he would step down, somehow having become wealthy during his tenure, and hand over the reins to a designated successor who would be nominated by the PRI and inevitably win.

By 1988 this system, like Mexico as a whole, was under strain. Salinas faced a real challenger: Cuauhtémoc Cárdenas, son of a popular former president, who countered Salinas's free-market reformism with a more traditional, anti-capitalist populism. It was a close election; Cárdenas won. But that was not how the official tally came out. Salinas became president; but now, more than any of his predecessors, he had to deliver the goods. And for that, he turned to his Cambridge-trained economic team.

The successes of the Salinas years were built on two crucial policy moves. First was a resolution of the debt crisis. In early 1989, its own presidential election safely past, the U.S. government began showing some unexpected willingness to face up to unpleasant realities. It finally admitted what everyone had long known, that many savings and loan associations had been gambling with taxpayer money and needed to be shut down; and, in a surprise speech, Treasury Secretary Nicholas Brady declared that Latin America's debt could not be fully repaid and that some kind of debt forgiveness would have to be worked out. The so-called Brady Plan was more a sentiment than an actual plan—Brady's speech emerged from bureaucratic intrigues worthy of *Yes, Minister,* during which those government officials who might have had the technical expertise to put together a workable blueprint for debt relief were kept in the dark, for fear that they might raise objections. But it gave the extremely competent Mexicans the opening they needed. Within a few months they had devised a scheme that was workable and that ended up replacing much of the outstanding debt with a smaller face value of "Brady bonds."

The overall debt relief from Mexico's Brady deal was modest, but it represented a psychological turning point. Mexicans who had long agitated for debt repudiation were mollified by seeing the foreign bankers give up a pound of flesh; the debt faded as a domestic political issue. Meanwhile foreign investors, who had been afraid to put funds into Mexico for fear that they would be trapped there, saw the deal as putting a period to that phase, and became ready to put in fresh money. The interest rates that Mexico had been forced to pay to keep money from fleeing the country plunged; and because the government no longer had to pay such high interest rates on its debt, the budget deficit quickly faded away. Within a year after the Brady deal, Mexico's financial situation had been transformed.

Nor was a settlement of the debt problem the only trick up Salinas's sleeve. In 1990 he astonished the world by proposing that Mexico establish free trade with the United States and Canada (which had already negotiated a free-trade agreement with each other). In quantitative terms the proposed North American Free Trade Agreement, or NAFTA, would matter less than one might have thought: the U.S. market was already fairly open to Mexican products, and the trade liberalization begun by de la Madrid had moved Mexico itself much, though not all, of the way to free trade. But like the debt reduction package, NAFTA was intended to mark a psychological turning point. By making Mexico's moves to open up to foreign goods and foreign investors not merely a domestic initiative but part of an international treaty, Salinas hoped to make those moves irreversible—and to convince the markets that they were irreversible. He also hoped to guarantee that Mexico's opening would be reciprocated, that the United States would in effect assure Mexico of access to its own market in perpetuity.

George Bush accepted Salinas's offer. How could he refuse? When the debt crisis struck in 1982, many in the United States had feared that the result would be a radicalization of Mexican politics, that anti-American forces—perhaps even Communists—would rise in the resulting chaos. Instead, pro-American, free-market types—our kind of people—had miraculously come to power, and offered to take down all the old barriers. To turn them down would be a slap in the face for reform; it would be practically to invite instability and hostility in our neighbor.

On compelling foreign-policy grounds, then, American diplomats were enthusiastic about NAFTA. Convincing Congress turned out to be a bit harder, as we will see. But in the first flush of enthusiasm, that was not yet apparent.

Instead, as the reforms in Mexico continued—as state enterprises were sold off, more import restrictions lifted, foreign investors welcomed—enthusiasm for Mexico's prospects accelerated. I personally recall talking to a group of multinational executives—heads of their companies' Latin American operations—in Cancún back in March 1993. I expressed some mild reservations about the Mexican situation, some evidence that the payoff to reform was a bit disappointing. "You're the only person in this room with anything negative to say about this country," I was politely informed. And people like those in the room put their money where their mouths were: in 1993 more than $30 billion in foreign capital was invested in Mexico.

Argentina's Break with the Past

"Rich as an Argentine." That was a common epithet in Europe before World War I, a time when Argentina was viewed by the public, and by investors, as a land of opportunity. Like Australia, Canada, and the United States, Argentina was a resource-rich nation, a favorite destination for both European emigrants and European capital. Buenos Aires was a gracious city with a European feel, hub of a first-rate British-built and -financed railway network, which gathered the wheat and meat of the pampas for export to the world. Linked by trade and investment to the global economy, by telegraph cable to the world capital market, Argentina was a member in good standing of the prewar international system.

True, even then Argentina had a certain tendency now and then to print too much money and to get into difficulties servicing its foreign debt. But then so did the United States. Few could have imagined that Argentina would eventually fall so far behind.

The interwar years were difficult for Argentina, as they were for all resource-exporting countries. The prices of agricultural products were low in the 1920s and crashed in the 1930s. And the situation was made worse by the debt run up in happier years. In effect, Argentina was like a farmer who borrowed heavily when times were good, and finds himself painfully squeezed between falling prices and fixed loan payments. Still, Argentina did not do as badly as one might have expected during the Depression. Its government proved less doctrinaire than those of advanced countries determined to defend the monetary proprieties at all costs. Thanks to a devalued peso, controls on capital flight, and a moratorium on debt repayment, Argentina was actually able to achieve a reasonably strong recovery after 1932; indeed, by 1934 Europeans were once again emigrating to Argentina, because they had a better prospect of finding jobs there than at home.

But the success of heterodox policies during the Depression helped establish governing habits that proved increasingly destructive as time went by. Emergency controls on foreign exchange became a nightmarishly complex set of regulations that discouraged enterprise and fostered corruption. Temporary limitations on imports became permanent barriers behind which astonishingly inefficient industries survived. Nationalized enterprises became sinks for public funds, employing hundreds of thousands of people yet failing to deliver essential services. And deficit spending repeatedly ran amok, leading to ever more disruptive bouts of inflation.

In the 1980s things went from bad to worse. After the debacle of the Falklands War in 1982, Argentina's military government had stepped down, and the civilian government of Raúl Alfonsín took power with the promise of economic revitalization. But the debt crisis struck Argentina as hard as the rest of Latin America, and Alfonsín's attempt to stabilize prices by introducing a new currency, the austral, failed dismally. By 1989 the nation was suffering from true hyperinflation, with prices rising at an annual rate of 3000 percent.

The victor in the 1989 election was Carlos Menem, the Peronist—that is, the candidate of the party founded by Juan

Perón, whose nationalistic and protectionist policies had done more than anything else to turn Argentina into a Third World nation. But Menem, it turned out, was prepared to do an economic version of Nixon's trip to China. As finance minster he appointed Domingo Cavallo, a Ph.D. from Harvard (of the same vintage as Mexico's Pedro Aspe); and Cavallo devised a reform plan even more radical than that of Mexico.

Part of the plan involved opening Argentina up to world markets—in particular, ending the long-standing, destructive habit of treating the country's agricultural exports as a cash cow, to be taxed at prohibitive rates in order to subsidize everything else. Privatization of the country's immense and utterly inefficient state-owned sector also proceeded at a rapid clip. (Unlike Mexico, Argentina even privatized the state-owned oil company.) Because Argentina's initial policies were arguably among the worst in the world, these reforms made a huge difference.

But the distinctive Cavallo touch was the monetary reform. In order to put a definitive end to the country's history of inflation, he resurrected a monetary system that had almost been forgotten in the modern world: a currency board.

Currency boards used to be standard in European colonial possessions. Such possessions would ordinarily be allowed to issue their own currency; but the currency would be rigidly tied in value to that of the mother country, and its soundness would be guaranteed by a law requiring that the domestic currency issue be fully backed by hard-currency reserves. That is, the public would be entitled to convert local currency into pounds or francs at a legally fixed rate, and the central bank would be obliged to keep enough of the mother country's currency on hand to exchange for all of the local notes.

In the postwar years, with the decline of colonial empires and the rise of active economic management, currency boards faded into oblivion. True, in 1983 Hong Kong, faced with a run on its currency, instituted a currency board pegging the Hong Kong dollar at 7.8 to the U.S. dollar. But Hong Kong was itself a sort of colonial relic, albeit a remarkably dynamic one, and the precedent attracted only limited attention.

Argentina's need for credibility, however, was desperate, and so Cavallo reached into the past. The ill-starred austral was replaced with a born-again peso, and this new peso was set at a permanently fixed exchange rate of one peso, one dollar—with every peso in circulation backed by a dollar of reserves. After decades of abusing its money, Argentina had, by law, renounced the ability to print money at all unless someone wanted to exchange a dollar for a peso.

The results were impressive. Inflation dropped rapidly to near zero. Like Mexico, Argentina negotiated a Brady deal and was rewarded with a resumption of capital inflow, though not on the same scale. And the real economy perked up dramatically: after years of decline, GDP increased by a quarter in just three years.

Mexico's Bad Year

At the end of 1993, were there any clouds on Latin America's horizon? Investors were euphoric: it seemed to them that the new free-market orientation of the continent had turned it into a land of opportunity. Foreign businessmen, like those I talked to in Cancún, were almost equally upbeat: the newly liberalized environment had created vast new opportunities for them. Only a few economists had questions, and these were relatively mild.

One question common to both Mexico and Argentina was the appropriateness of the exchange rate. Both countries had stabilized their currencies; both had brought inflation down; but in both cases the slowdown in inflation lagged behind the stabilization of the exchange rate. In Argentina, for example, the peso was pegged against the dollar in 1991; yet over the next two years consumer prices rose 40 percent, compared with only 6 in the United States. A similar, if less stark, process occurred in Mexico; in both cases the effect was to make the country's goods expensive on world markets, leading economists to wonder if their currencies had become overvalued.

A related question involved the trade balance (more accurately, the current account balance, a broader measure that includes services, payment of interest, and so on — but I will use the terms interchangeably). In the early 1990s Mexico's exports grew rather slowly, mainly because the strong peso made their prices uncompetitive. At the same time imports, pulled in both by the removal of import barriers and by a boom in credit, surged. The result was a huge excess of imports over exports: by 1993 Mexico's deficit had reached 8 percent of GDP, a number with few historical precedents. Was this a sign of trouble?

Mexican officials, and many outside the country, argued that it was not. Their argument came straight out of the economics textbooks. As a sheer matter of accounting, the balance of payments always balances: that is, every purchase that a country makes from foreigners must be matched by a sale of equal value. (Economics students know that there is a small technical qualification to this statement involving unrequited transfers; never mind.) If a country is running a deficit on its *current* account — buying more goods than it sells — it must correspondingly be running an equal surplus on its *capital* account — selling more *assets* than it buys. And the converse is equally true: a country that runs a surplus on capital account must run a deficit on current account. But that meant that Mexico's success in getting foreigners to bring their money, to buy Mexican assets, had a trade deficit as its necessary counterpart — the deficit, in fact, was simply another way of saying that foreigners thought Mexico was a great place to invest. The only reason to be concerned, said the optimists, would be if the capital inflow were somehow artificial — if the government were pulling capital in from abroad by borrowing the money itself (as it did before 1982) or by running budget deficits that created a shortage of domestic savings. Mexico's government, however, was running a balanced budget and was actually building up overseas assets (foreign exchange reserves) rather than liabilities. So why be concerned? If the private sector wanted to pour capital into Mexico, why should the government try to stop it?

And yet there was a disturbing aspect of Mexico's performance: given all the reforms, and all that capital coming in, where was the growth?

Between 1981 and 1989 the Mexican economy had grown at an annual rate of only 1.3 percent, well short of population growth, leaving per capita income far below its 1981 peak. From 1990 to 1994, the years of the "Mexican miracle," things were definitely better: the economy grew 2.8 percent per year. But this was still barely ahead of population growth; as of 1994 Mexico was still, according to its own statistics, far below its 1981 level. Where was the miracle—indeed, where was the payoff to all those reforms, all that foreign investment? In 1993 the MIT economist Rudiger Dornbusch, a longtime observer of the Mexican economy (and the teacher of many of the economists now running Mexico, Aspe included), wrote a caustic analysis of the situation entitled "Mexico: Stabilization, Reform, and No Growth."

Defenders of the Mexican record argued that these numbers failed to reveal the true progress of the economy, especially the transformation from an inefficient, inward-looking industrial base to a highly competitive export orientation. Still, it was certainly disturbing that the huge capital inflows were producing so little measurable result. What was going wrong?

Dornbusch and others argued that the problem lay in the value of the peso: an excessively strong currency was pricing Mexican goods out of world markets, preventing the economy from taking advantage of its growing capacity. What Mexico needed, then, was a devaluation—a onetime reduction in the dollar value of the peso, which would get its economy moving again. After all, in 1992 Britain had been forced by the financial markets (and in particular by George Soros—see Chapter 7) to let the value of the pound decline, and the result was to turn a recession into a boom. Mexico, said some, needed a dose of the same medicine. (Similar arguments were also made for Argentina, whose growth had been much faster than Mexico's, but which faced stubbornly high unemployment.)

The Mexicans dismissed such talk, assuring investors that their economic program was on track, that they saw no reason to devalue the peso, and that they had no intention of doing so.

It was particularly important to put up a good front because the North American Free Trade Agreement required approval from the U.S. Congress and had run into stiff opposition. Ross Perot had memorably warned of the "great sucking sound" the United States would hear as all its jobs moved south; more respectable voices offered more respectable-sounding arguments. During 1993 the Clinton administration, which had inherited NAFTA from its predecessor, pulled out all the stops and with great difficulty secured passage; but it was a pretty close thing—and just in time.

For during the course of 1994 some important things started to go wrong in Mexico. On New Year's Day there was a peasant uprising in the poor rural state of Chiapas, an area that had gone untouched economically or politically by the changes sweeping through much of Mexico. The stability of the government was not threatened, but the incident was a reminder that bad old habits of corruption, and grinding rural poverty, were still very much a part of the Mexican scene. More serious was the March assassination of Donaldo Colosio, Salinas's designated successor. Colosio was a rare combination of reformer and charismatic popular politician, widely regarded as just the man to truly legitimize the new way of doing things; his assassination both deprived the country of a much needed leader and suggested that dark forces (corrupt political bosses? drug lords?) did not want a strong reformer in charge. The replacement candidate, Ernesto Zedillo, was an American-trained economist whose honesty and intelligence were not in question; but was he a political naïf who would allow himself to be bullied by the dinosaurs? Finally, in the run-up to the election the PRI set about trying to buy support with a moderately large spending spree; some of the pesos it printed were converted into dollars, draining the foreign exchange reserves.

Zedillo won the election, fairly this time, because he managed to convince voters that the populist views of Cárdenas would provoke a financial crisis—as one Mexican friend put it to me, the PRI convinced the voters that unless they voted for

Zedillo, "what did happen, would happen." For, alas, the financial crisis came anyway.

The Tequila Crisis

In December 1994, faced with a steady drain on their reserves of foreign exchange, Mexican authorities had to decide what to do. They could stem the loss by raising interest rates, thereby making it attractive for Mexican residents to keep their money in pesos, and perhaps attracting in foreign funds as well. But this rise in interest rates would hurt business and consumer spending, and Mexico was, after several years of disappointing growth, already on the edge of a recession. Or they could devalue the peso—reduce its value in terms of dollars—hoping that this would have the same effect as in Britain sixteen months earlier. That is, a devaluation could in the best scenario not only make Mexico's exports more competitive but also convince foreign investors that Mexican assets were good value, and hence actually allow interest rates to fall.

Mexico chose devaluation. But it botched the job.

What is supposed to happen when a country's currency is devalued is that speculators say, "Okay, that's over," and stop betting on the currency's continued decline. That is the way it worked for Britain and Sweden in 1992. The danger is that speculators will instead view the first devaluation as a sign of more to come, and start speculating all the harder. In order to avoid that, a government is supposed to follow certain rules. First, if you devalue at all, make the devaluation big enough. Otherwise, you will simply set up expectations of more to come. Second, immediately following the devaluation you must give every signal you can that everything is under control, that you are responsible people who understand the importance of treating investors right, and so on. Otherwise the devaluation can crystallize doubts about your economy's soundness and start a panic.

Mexico broke both rules. The initial devaluation was 15 percent, only half of what economists like Dornbusch had been suggesting. And the behavior of government officials was anything but reassuring. The new finance minister, Jaime Serra Puche, appeared arrogant and indifferent to the opinion of foreign creditors; worse yet, it soon became clear that some Mexican businessmen had been consulted about the devaluation in advance, giving them inside information denied to foreign investors. Massive capital flight was now inevitable, and the Mexican government soon had to abandon fixing the exchange rate at all.

Still, Serra Puche was quickly replaced, and Mexico began making all the right noises; and one might have thought that all the reforms since 1985 would count for something. But no: foreign investors were shocked—shocked!—to discover that Mexico was not the paragon it had seemed, and wanted out at any cost. Soon the peso had fallen to half its pre-crisis value.

The most pressing problem was the government's own budget. Governments whose financial credibility is suspect have trouble selling long-term bonds and usually end up with substantial amounts of short-term debt that must be rolled over at frequent intervals. Mexico was no exception; and the need to pay high interest rates on that debt was a major source of fiscal problems in the 1980s. As we saw, one of the big benefits of the Brady deal of 1989 was that by making investors more confident it allowed Mexico to roll over its short-term debt at much reduced interest rates. Now these gains were lost, and more: by March Mexico was paying 75 percent in order to persuade investors to keep their money there.

Worse yet, in an effort to convince the markets that it would not devalue, Mexico had converted billions of short-term debt into so-called *tesobonos*, which were indexed to the dollar; as the peso plunged, the size of these dollarized debts exploded. And as the *tesobono* problem received wide publicity, it only reinforced the sense of panic.

The government's financial crisis soon spilled over into the private sector. During 1995 Mexico's real GDP would plunge 7 percent, its industrial production 15 percent, far worse than anything the United States has seen since the 1930s—indeed, far worse than the initial slump that followed the 1982 debt crisis. Thousands of businesses went bankrupt; hundreds of thousands of workers lost their jobs. Exactly why the financial crisis had such a devastating effect on the real economy—and why the Mexican government could not, baby-sitting-co-op style, act to prevent that slump—is a key question. But let us postpone that discussion until we have a few more crises under our belt.

Most startling of all, the crisis was not confined to Mexico. Instead, the "tequila effect" spread across much of the world, and in particular to other Latin America countries, especially Argentina.

This was an unpleasant surprise. For one thing, Argentina and Mexico are at the opposite ends of Latin America, with few direct trade or financial links. Moreover, Argentina's currency board system was supposed to make the credibility of *its* peso invulnerable. How could it be caught up in Mexico's crisis?

Perhaps Argentina was attacked because to Yanqui investors all Latin American nations look alike. But once speculation against the Argentine peso began, it became clear that the currency board did not provide the kind of insulation its creators had hoped for. True, every peso in circulation was backed by a dollar in reserves, so that in a mechanical sense the country could always defend the peso's value. But what would happen when the public, rationally or not, began to change large numbers of pesos into dollars? The answer, it turned out, was that the country's banks moved quickly to the edge of collapse and threatened to bring the rest of the economy down with them.

Here's how it worked: suppose that a New York loan officer, made nervous by the news from Mexico, decides that he had better reduce his Latin American exposure—and that it is not worth trying to explain to his boss that, as Ronald Reagan once remarked, "they're all different countries." So he tells an Argentine client that his credit line will not be renewed and that the outstanding balance must be repaid. The client withdraws the necessary pesos from his local bank, converting them into dollars with no trouble, because the central bank has plenty of dollars on hand. But the Argentine bank must now replenish its cash reserves; so it calls in a loan to an Argentine businessman.

That's where the trouble starts. To repay its loan, the business must acquire pesos, which will probably be withdrawn from an account at some other Argentine bank—which will itself therefore have to call in some loans, leading to more bank withdrawals, leading to further reductions in credit. The initial reduction in lending from abroad, in other words, will have a *multiplied* effect within Argentina: each dollar of reduced credit from New York leads to several pesos of called loans in Buenos Aires.

And as credit contracts, the business situation in Argentina starts to become dicey. Businesses have trouble repaying their loans on short notice, all the more so because their customers are also under financial pressure. Depositors start to wonder whether banks can really collect from their clients, and start to pull their money out just in case, further tightening credit conditions . . . and we have the beginnings of the sort of vicious circle of credit crunch and bank run that devastated the U.S. economy in 1930–31.

Now, modern nations have defenses against that sort of thing. First of all, deposits are insured by the government, so depositors are not supposed to worry. Second, the central bank is prepared to act as "lender of last resort," rushing cash to banks so they aren't forced into desperate fire-sale methods to meet the demands of depositors. Argentina should thus have been able to nip this process in the bud.

But things weren't that easy. Argentine depositors may have believed that their pesos were safe, but they were less sure that they would preserve their value in dollars; so they wanted to make sure by getting into dollars now, just in case. And the central bank couldn't act as lender of last resort, because it was prohibited from printing new pesos except in exchange for dollars! The very rules designed to protect the system from one kind of crisis of confidence left it deeply vulnerable to another.

In early 1995, then, both Mexico and Argentina went suddenly from euphoria to terror: it seemed all too likely that the reformist experiments in both countries would end in disastrous collapse.

The Great Rescue

What Latin America needed, urgently, was dollars: dollars with which Mexico could repay the *tesobonos* as they came due, dollars that would allow Argentina to print pesos and lend them to its banks.

The Mexican package was the larger, more urgent, and politically more difficult of the two. While much of the money came from international agencies like the International Monetary Fund, Europe and Japan saw a Mexican rescue as mainly a U.S. issue, and the United States therefore would have to provide a large chunk of the money itself. Unfortunately, there were powerful political forces arrayed against any such rescue. Those who had bitterly opposed NAFTA saw the Mexican crisis as vindication and were not about to see taxpayers' money used to bail out the Mexicans and the bankers who had lent them money. Meanwhile, conservatives disliked the whole idea of governments intervening to support markets, and particularly disliked the role of the International Monetary Fund, which they regarded as a step on the way toward world government. It soon became clear that the U.S. Congress would not approve any funding for a Mexican rescue.

Luckily, it turned out that the U.S. Treasury can at its own discretion make use of the Exchange Stabilization Fund (ESF), a pot of money set aside for emergency intervention in foreign exchange markets. The intent of the legislation that established that fund was clearly to stabilize the value of the *dollar*; but the language didn't actually say that. So with admirable creativity Treasury used it to stabilize the peso instead. Between the ESF and other sources, a remarkable $50 billion credit line was quickly made available to Mexico; and after several heart-pounding months the financial situation did indeed begin to stabilize.

Argentina's lower-profile rescue came via the World Bank,

which put up $12 billion to support the nation's banks.

The rescues for Mexico and Argentina did not prevent a very severe economic contraction—considerably worse, in fact, than what happened in the first year of the 1980s debt crisis. But by late 1995 investors began to calm down, to believe that maybe the countries were not going to collapse after all. Interest rates came down; spending started to revive; and soon Mexico and Argentina were both making a rapid recovery. For thousands of businesses and millions of workers, the crisis had been devastating; but it ended sooner than most had feared or expected.

Learning the Wrong Lessons

Two years after the tequila crisis, it seemed as if everything was back on track. Both Mexico and Argentina were booming; those investors who had kept their nerve did very well indeed. And so, perversely, what might have been seen as a warning instead became, if anything, a source of complacency. While few people laid out the lessons learned from the Latin crisis explicitly, an informal summary of the post-tequila conventional wisdom might have run as follows:

First, the tequila crisis was not about the way the world at large works: it was a case of Mexico being Mexico. It was caused by Mexican policy errors—notably, allowing the currency to become overvalued, expanding credit instead of tightening it when speculation against the peso began, and botching the devaluation itself in a way that unnerved investors. And the depth of the slump that followed had mainly to do with the uniquely tricky political economy of the Mexican situation, with its still-unresolved legacy of populism and anti-Americanism; in a way you could say that the slump was punishment for the theft of the 1988 election.

The lesson taken, in short, was that Mexico's debacle was of little relevance to the rest of the world. True, the crisis had spilled over to the rest of Latin America; but Argentina's brush with financial collapse somehow did not fully register on the world's attention, perhaps because it was followed by such a strong recovery. And surely the tequila crisis would not be replicated in well-run economies without a history of macroeconomic populism—countries like the miracle economies of Asia.

The other lesson concerned not Mexico but Washington— that is, the International Monetary Fund and the U.S. Treasury Department. What the crisis seemed to show was that Washington had things under control: that it had the resources and the knowledge to contain even severe financial crises. Huge aid was quickly mobilized on Mexico's behalf; and it did the trick. Instead of the seven lean years of the 1980s, the tequila crisis was over in a year and a half. Clearly, it seemed, the people in charge had gotten better at this sort of thing.

Four years after the tequila crisis began, with the terrible experience of Asia fresh in our memories and Brazil's economy spiraling out of control, it was clear that we learned the wrong lessons from Latin America.

What we should have asked was the question posed in many meetings by the economist Guillermo Calvo, of the World Bank and later of the University of Maryland: "Why was so large a punishment imposed for so small a crime?" In the aftermath of the tequila crisis it was all too easy to revisit the policies followed by Mexico in the run-up to that crisis, and find them full of error; but the fact was that at the time they seemed pretty good, and even after the fact it was hard to find any missteps large enough to justify the economic catastrophe of 1995. We should have taken Calvo's question—with its implication that there were mechanisms transforming minor policy mistakes into major economic disasters—to heart. We should have looked more closely at the arguments of some commentators that there really were no serious mistakes at all, except for the brief series of fumbles that got Mexico on the wrong side of market perceptions, and set in motion a process of self-justifying panic. And we should therefore also have realized that what happened to Mexico could happen elsewhere: that the seeming success of an economy, the admiration of markets and media for its managers, was no guarantee that the economy was immune to sudden financial crisis.

In retrospect it is also clear that we gave far too much credit to "Washington," to the IMF and the Treasury. It was true that they had acted courageously and decisively, and that the results had been a vindication. But on close examination the omens were not all that good for a repeat performance. For one thing, the mobilization of money was achieved through what amounted to a legal sleight of hand, justified mainly by the special significance of Mexico to U.S. interests; money would not come as quickly or as easily in later crises. The Mexican rescue was also made less complicated by the cooperation of the Mexican government: Zedillo's people had no pride to swallow—not with Mexico's history—and were in complete agreement with Washington about what needed to be done. Dealing with Asian countries that had been accustomed to negotiating from a position of strength, and with Asian leaders accustomed to having things their own way, would be very different.

Perhaps most of all, we failed to understand the extent to which both Mexico and Washington simply got lucky. The rescue wasn't really a well-considered plan that addressed the essence of the crisis: it was an emergency injection of cash to a beleaguered government, which did its part by adopting painful measures less because they were clearly related to the economic problems than because by demonstrating the government's seriousness they might restore market confidence. They succeeded, albeit only after the economy had been punished severely; but there was no good reason to suppose that such a strategy would work the next time.

And so nobody was prepared either for the emergence of a new, tequila-style crisis in Asia, or for the ineffectiveness of a Mexican-style rescue when that crisis came. What was odd about our obliviousness was that Asia's biggest economy was already in serious trouble—and was doing a notably bad job job taking care of its own business.

F O U R

■

The Future That Didn't
Work: Japan in the 1990s

ONLY yesterday, it seems, Americans were obsessed
with Japan. The successes of Japanese industry inspired both
admiration and fear; you couldn't enter an airport bookstore
without encountering rows of dust jackets featuring rising suns
and samurai warriors. Some of these books promised to teach
the secrets of Japanese management; others prophesied (or
demanded) economic warfare. As role models or demons, or
both, the Japanese were very much on our minds.

All that is gone now. There is an occasional flurry of excite-
ment mingled with schadenfreude as another big Japanese
bank fails, or as the Nikkei falls another few percent. But for the
most part we have lost interest. They weren't that tough after
all, the public seems to have concluded, so now we can ignore
them.

This is foolish. The failures of Japan are every bit as significant for us as its successes. What has happened to Japan is both
a tragedy and an omen. The world's second-largest economy is
still blessed with well-educated and willing workers, a modern
capital stock, and impressive technological know-how. It has a

stable government, which has no difficulty collecting taxes; unlike Latin America, or for that matter smaller Asian economies, it is a creditor nation, not dependent on the good-will of foreign investors. And the sheer size of its economy, which means that its producers sell mainly to the domestic market, should give Japan — like the United States — a freedom of action denied to lesser nations.

Yet Japan has spent most of the past decade in a slump, alter-nating brief and inadequate periods of economic growth with ever-deeper recessions. Once the growth champion of the advanced world, in 1998 Japanese industry produced less than it had in 1991. And even worse than the performance itself is the sense of fatalism and helplessness: Japan's public no longer appears to expect its economic managers to turn the situation around, nor do those managers themselves seem to believe that they can do much about the situation.

This is a tragedy: a great economy like this does not need or deserve to be in a permanent slump. Japan's woes are not as acute as those of other Asian nations, but they have gone on far longer, with far less justification. It is also an omen: if it can happen to them, who is to say that it can't happen to us?

How did it happen?

Japan as Number One

No country — not even the Soviet Union in the days of Stalin's five-year plans — had ever experienced as stunning an econom-ic transformation as Japan did in the high-growth years from 1953 to 1973. In the space of two decades a largely agricultur-al nation became the world's largest exporter of steel and auto-mobiles, greater Tokyo became the world's largest and arguably most vibrant metropolitan area, and the standard of living made a quantum leap.

Some Westerners took notice. As early as 1969 the futurist Herman Kahn published *The Emerging Japanese Superstate*, predicting that Japan's high growth rates would make it the world's leading economy by the year 2000. But it was not until

THE RETURN OF DEPRESSION ECONOMICS

the late 1970s—around the time that Ezra Vogel wrote his best-seller, *Japan as Number One*—that the realization of just how much Japan had achieved really dawned on the wider public. As sophisticated Japanese products—above all, automobiles and consumer electronics—flooded into Western markets, people began to wonder about the secret of Japan's success.

There is a certain irony in the timing of the great debate about Japan. The funny thing was that the heroic age of Japanese economic growth ended just about the time Westerners started to take Japan seriously. In the early 1970s, for reasons that are still a bit mysterious, growth slowed throughout the advanced world. Japan, which had had the highest growth rate, also experienced the biggest slowdown—from 9 percent a year in the 1960s to less than 4 percent after 1973. Although this rate was still faster than that of any other advanced country (half again as fast as that of the United States), at that rate the date of Japan's emergence as the world's leading economy would have to be put off well into the twenty-first century. Still, Japan's growth performance was, literally, the envy of other nations; many people argued not only that Japan had figured out a better way to run its economy but that its success came at least partly at the expense of naive Western competitors.

We need not replay here the whole debate over why Japan was successful. Basically, there were two sides. One side explained the growth as the product of good fundamentals, above all excellent basic education and a high savings rate, and—as always—also engaged in a bit of amateur sociology to explain why Japan was so very good at manufacturing high-quality products at low cost. The other side argued that Japan had developed a fundamentally different economic system, a new and superior form of capitalism. And the debate over Japan also became a debate over economics, over the validity of Western economic thought in general and the virtues of free markets in particular.

One element of the supposedly superior Japanese system was government guidance. In the fifties and sixties the Japanese government—both the famed Ministry of International Trade and Industry (MITI) and the quieter but even more influential Ministry of Finance—played a strong role in directing the economy. Bank loans and import licenses flowed to favored industries and firms; the economy's growth was at least partly channeled by the government's strategic designs. By the time the West really focused on Japan, the government's grip had been much loosened; but the image of "Japan Inc.," a centrally directed economy bent on dominating world markets, remained a potent one into the 1990s.

Another element of the distinctive Japanese economic style was the insulation of major companies from short-term financial pressures. Members of Japanese *keiretsu*—groups of allied firms organized around a main bank—typically owned substantial quantities of each other's shares, making management largely independent of the outside stockholders. Nor did Japanese companies worry too much about stock prices, or market confidence, since they rarely financed themselves by selling either stocks or bonds; instead, the main bank lent them the money they needed. So Japanese firms did not have to worry about short-term profitability, or indeed to worry much about profitability at all. One might have thought that the financial condition of the bank would in the end discipline the *keiretsu's* investment: if the loans looked unsound, wouldn't the bank start to lose depositors? But in Japan as in most countries, depositors believed that the government would never allow them to lose their savings, so they paid little attention to what the banks did with their money.

The result of this system, claimed both those who admired it and those who feared it, was a country able to take the long view. One by one, the Japanese government would target "strategic" industries, those that could serve as engines of growth. The private sector would be guided into those industries, helped along by an initial period of protection from foreign competition, during which the industry could hone its skills in the domestic market. Then would come the great export drive, during which firms would ignore profitability while building market share and driving their foreign competitors into the ground. Eventually, its dominance of the industry secured, Japan would move on to the next one. Steel, autos, VCRs, semiconductors—soon it would be computers and aircraft.

Skeptics poked holes in many of the details of this account. But even those who absolved Japan of the charge of predatory behavior, who questioned whether the wizards of MITI were really as all-knowing as advertised, tended to agree that the distinctive characteristics of the Japanese system must have something to do with Japanese success. Only much later would those same distinctive characteristics—the cozy relationship between government and business, the extension of easy credit by government-guaranteed banks to closely allied companies—come to be labeled crony capitalism and seen as the root of economic malaise.

But the weaknesses of the system were actually evident by the late 1980s, to anyone willing to see.

Bubble, Toil and Trouble

At the beginning of 1990 the market capitalization of Japan—the total value of all the stocks of all the nation's companies—was larger than that of the United States, which had twice Japan's population and more than twice its gross domestic product. Land, never cheap in crowded Japan, had become incredibly expensive: according to a widely cited factoid, the land underneath the square mile of Tokyo's Imperial Palace was worth more than the entire state of California. Welcome to the "bubble economy," Japan's equivalent of the Roaring Twenties.

The late 1980s were a time of prosperity for Japan, of fast growth, low unemployment, and high profits. Nonetheless, nothing in the underlying economic data justified the tripling of both land and stock prices in the late 1980s. Even at the time many observers thought that there was something manic and irrational about the financial boom—that traditional companies in slowly growing industries should not be valued like growth stocks, with price-earnings ratios of 60 or more. But as is so often the case in manic markets, the skeptics were without the resources, or the courage, to back their lack of conviction; conventional wisdom found all sorts of justifications for the sky-high prices.

Financial bubbles are nothing new. From tulip mania to Internet mania, even the most sensible investors have found it hard to resist getting caught up in the momentum, to take a long view when everyone else is getting rich. But given the reputation of the Japanese for long-term strategic thinking, the common perception that Japan Inc. was more like a planned economy than a free-market free-for-all, the extent of the bubble remains somewhat surprising.

It does turn out that Japan's reputation for long-sighted, socially controlled investment has always exaggerated the reality. Real estate speculators, often getting an extra edge by paying off politicians, and another extra edge through *yakuza* connections, have been a surprisingly important part of the Japanese scene for as long as anyone can remember. Speculative investments in real estate came close to provoking a banking crisis in the 1970s; the situation was saved only through a burst of inflation, which reduced the real value of the speculators' debts and turned bad loans good again. Still, the sheer extent of Japan's bubble was astonishing. Was there some explanation of the phenomenon that ran beyond mere crowd psychology?

Well, it turns out that Japan's bubble was only one of several outbreaks of speculative fever around the world during the 1980s. All of these outbreaks had the common feature that they were financed mainly by bank loans—in particular, that traditionally staid institutions started offering credit to risk-loving, even shady operators in return for somewhat above-market interest rates. The most famous case was that of America's savings and loan associations—institutions whose public image used to be defined by the all-American earnestness of Jimmy Stewart's small-town banker in *It's a Wonderful Life*, but which in the 1980s became identified instead with high-rolling Texas real estate moguls. But similar outbreaks of dubious lending occurred elsewhere, notably in Sweden, another country not usually identified with speculative fever. And economists have long argued that behind all such episodes lies the same economic principle—one of those principles, like the basic baby-sitting model of a recession, that will reappear several times in this book. The principle is known as moral hazard.

The term "moral hazard" has its origins in the insurance industry. Very early in the game providers of fire insurance, in particular, noticed that property owners who were fully insured against loss had an interesting tendency to have destructive fires—particularly when changing conditions had reduced the probable market value of their building to less than the insurance coverage. (In the mid-1980s New York City had a number of known "arson-prone" landlords, some of whom would buy a building at an inflated price from a dummy company they themselves owned, use that price as the basis for a large insurance policy, then just happen to have a fire. Moral hazard, indeed.) Eventually the term came to refer to any situation in which one person makes the decision about how much risk to take, while someone else bears the cost if things go badly.

Borrowed money is inherently likely to produce moral hazard. Suppose that I were a smart guy, but without any capital; and that based on my evident cleverness you decided to lend me a billion dollars, to invest any way I see fit, as long as I promise to repay in a year's time. Even if you charge me a high rate of interest, this is a great deal: I will take the billion, put it into something that *might* make a lot of money, but then again might end up worthless, and hope for the best. If the investment prospers, so will I; if it does not, I will declare personal bankruptcy, and walk away. Heads I win, tails you lose.

Of course, that is why nobody will lend someone without capital of his own a billion dollars to invest as he sees fit, no matter how smart he may seem. Creditors normally place restrictions on what borrowers can do with any money they lend; and borrowers are also normally obliged to put up substantial amounts of their own money, in order to give them a good reason to avoid losses.

Sometimes lenders seem to forget about these rules, and

lend large sums no questions asked to people who put on a good show of knowing what they are doing; we'll get to the amazing story of the hedge funds in Chapter 7. At other times the requirement that the borrower put up enough of his own money can itself be a source of market instability. When assets lose value, those who bought them with borrowed money can be faced with a "margin call": they must either put more of their own money in or repay their creditors by selling the assets, driving the prices down still further, a process that has been central to the financial crises of the last two years. But leaving such market pathologies aside, there is another, more systematic reason why the rules sometimes get broken: because the moral hazard game is played at taxpayers' expense.

Remember what we said about the main banks of Japanese *keiretsu*: that their depositors believe their deposits to be safe, because the government stands behind them. The same is true of almost all banks in the First World, and most banks elsewhere. Modern nations, even if they do not explicitly guarantee deposits, cannot find it in their hearts to let widows and orphans lose their life savings simply because they put them in the wrong bank, just as they cannot bring themselves to stand aside when the raging river sweeps away houses foolishly built in the flood plain. Only the most hard-nosed of conservatives would wish it otherwise; but the result is that people are careless about where they build their houses, and even more careless about where they store their money.

This carelessness offers a nice opportunity to an unscrupulous businessman. Just open a bank, making sure that it has an impressive building and a fancy name. Attract a lot of deposits, by paying good interest if that is allowed, by offering toasters or whatever if it isn't. Then lend the money out, at high interest rates, to high-rolling speculators (preferably friends of yours, or maybe even yourself behind a different corporate front). The depositors won't ask about the quality of your investments, since they know that they are protected in any case. And you now have a one-way option: if the investments do well, you become rich; if they do badly, you can simply walk away and let the government clean up the mess.

Okay, it's not that easy, because government regulators aren't entirely stupid. In fact, from the 1930s to the 1980s this kind of behavior was quite rare among bankers, because regulators did more or less the same things that a private lender would do before handing me a billion dollars to play with. They restricted what banks could do with depositors' money, in an effort to prevent excessive risk-taking. They required that the owners of banks put substantial amounts of their own money at stake, through capital requirements. And in a more subtle, perhaps unintentional measure, regulators have historically limited the amount of competition among banks, making a banking license a valuable thing in itself, possessed of a considerable "franchise value"; licensees were loath to jeopardize this franchise value by taking risks that could break the bank.

But in the 1980s these restraints broke down in many places. Mainly the cause was deregulation. Traditional banks were safe, but also very conservative; arguably they failed to direct capital to its most productive uses. The cure, argued reformers, was both more freedom and more competition: let banks lend where they thought best, and allow more players to compete for public savings. Somehow it got forgotten that this would give banks more freedom to take bad risks and that by reducing their franchise value it would give them less incentive to avoid them. Changes in the marketplace, notably the rise of alternative sources of corporate finance, further eroded the profit margins of bankers who clung to safe, old-fashioned ways of doing businesses.

And so in the 1980s there was a sort of global epidemic of moral hazard. Few countries can be proud of their handling of the situation—surely not the United States, whose mishandling of the savings and loan affair was a classic case of imprudent, shortsighted, and occasionally corrupt policymaking. But Japan, where all the usual lines—between government and business, between banks and their clients, between what was and what was not subject to government guarantee—were especially blurry, was peculiarly ill suited to a loosened financial regime. Japan's banks lent more, with less regard for quality of the borrower, than anyone else's; and in so doing they helped inflate the bubble economy to grotesque proportions.

Sooner or later, such bubbles do burst. The bursting of the Japanese bubble, it turns out, was not entirely spontaneous: the Bank of Japan, concerned about speculative excess, began raising interest rates in 1990 in an effort to let some of the air out of the balloon. At first this policy was unsuccessful; but beginning in 1991 land and stock prices began a steep decline, which within a few years put them some 60 percent below their peak.

Initially, and indeed for several years thereafter, Japanese authorities seem to have regarded all of this as healthy—a return to more sensible, realistic asset valuations. But it gradually became apparent that the end of the bubble economy had brought not economic health but a steadily deepening malaise.

A Stealthy Depression

Unlike Mexico in 1995, or South Korea in 1998, Japan has never (yet?) gone through a year of unmistakable, catastrophic economic decline. In the eight years since the bubble burst, Japan's real GDP has contracted in only two. Unemployment has risen only gradually, and still does not seem very high by Western standards (although that is largely a measurement issue: when women or older workers, who are last-hired-first-fired in Japan, are unable to find jobs, they are not usually counted as unemployed; by American standards Japan would probably now have an unemployment rate close to 10 percent).

But year after year growth fell short not just of the economy's previous experience but of any reasonable estimate of the growth in its capacity. In only one year after 1991 did Japan grow as fast as it did in an *average* year in the preceding decade. And even if you thought that the rate of growth of Japan's "potential" output—the output that it could have produced with full employment of its resources—had suddenly fallen to half its pre-1991 level, that brief burst of growth in 1996 was also the only year in which actual output grew as fast as potential.

Economists have one of their famously awkward phrases for what Japan was experiencing: a "growth recession." A growth recession is what happens when an economy grows, but not fast enough to make use of the increases in its capacity, so that more and more machines and workers stand idle. Normally growth recessions are rather rare, because both booms and slumps tend to gather momentum, producing either rapid growth or clear-cut decline. Japan, however, has essentially experienced an eight-year growth recession, which has left it so far below where it ought to be that it verges on a new phenomenon: a growth depression.

The slowness with which Japan's economy has deteriorated is in itself a source of much confusion. Because the depression crept up on the country, there was never (until last year) a moment at which the public clamored for the government to do something dramatic. Because Japan's economic engine gradually lost power rather than coming to a screeching halt, the government itself has consistently defined success down, regarding the economy's continuing growth as a vindication of its policies even though that growth was well short of what could and should have been achieved. (At the time of writing, Japanese officials were trumpeting their success—via massive public works spending—at generating slightly positive growth in the fourth quarter of 1998, as if that represented a fundamental turnaround.) And at the same time, both Japanese and foreign analysts have tended to assume that because Japan has grown so slowly for so long, it *cannot* grow any faster.

So Japan's economic policies have been marked by an odd combination of smugness and fatalism—and by a noticeable unwillingness to think hard about how things can have gone so very wrong.

Japan's Trap

There is nothing mysterious about the onset of Japan's slump in 1991: sooner or later the financial bubble was bound to burst, and when it did it would bring about a decline in investment, in consumption, and hence in overall demand. If the U.S. stock market were to crash tomorrow (if it hasn't already by the time this book is published), the effect would probably be a slowdown, maybe even a brief recession in the U.S. economy. The operative word, however, is "brief": surely Alan Greenspan would do what was necessary to get the economy moving again. And even more surely, there would be no reason to be fatalistic about the situation, to regard a prolonged hangover from the earlier excesses as somehow inevitable.

It is time to return to the story of the baby-sitting co-op. Suppose that the U.S. stock market were to crash, threatening to undermine consumer confidence. Would this inevitably mean a disastrous recession? Think of it this way: when consumer confidence declines, it is as if for some reason the typical member of the co-op had become less willing to go out, more anxious to accumulate coupons for a rainy day. This could indeed lead to a slump—but need not, if the management were alert and responded by simply issuing more coupons. That is exactly what our head coupon issuer, Alan Greenspan, did in 1987, and what I believe he would do again.

Or suppose that Greenspan did not respond quickly enough, and that the economy did indeed fall into a slump. Don't panic: even if the head coupon issuer has gotten temporarily behind the curve, he can still ordinarily turn the situation around by issuing more coupons—that is, with a vigorous monetary expansion, like the ones that ended the recessions of 1981–82 and 1990–91.

What about all the bad investments made during the boom? Well, that was so much wasted capital. But there is no obvious reason why bad investments made in the past require an actual slump in output in the present. Capacity may not have risen as much as anticipated, but it has not actually fallen; why not just print enough money to keep spending up, so that the economy makes full use of the capacity it has?

Remember, the story of the co-op tells you that economic slumps are not punishments for our sins, pains that we are fated to suffer. The Capitol Hill co-op did not get into trouble because its members were bad, inefficient baby-sitters; its troubles did not reveal the fundamental flaws of "Capitol Hill values" or "crony baby-sittingism." It had a technical problem—too many people chasing too little scrip—which could be, and was, solved with a little clear thinking. And so the co-op's story ought to inoculate us against fatalism and pessimism; it seems to imply that recessions are always, and indeed easily, curable.

But in that case why didn't Japan pull up its socks after the bubble burst? How can Japan be stuck in a seemingly intractable slump—one that it does not appear able to get out of simply by printing coupons? Well, if we extend the co-op's story a little bit, it is not hard to generate something that looks a lot like Japan's problems—and to see the outline of a solution.

First, we have to imagine a co-op whose members realized that there was an unnecessary inconvenience in their system: there would be occasions when a couple found itself needing to go out several times in a row, and would run out of coupons—and therefore would be unable to get its babies sat—even though it was entirely willing to do lots of compensatory baby-sitting at a later date. To resolve this problem, the co-op allowed members to *borrow* extra coupons from the management in times of need—repaying with the coupons received from subsequent baby-sitting. (We could move the story a bit closer to the way real economies work by imagining that couples could also borrow coupons from each other; the interest rate in this infant capital market would then play the role the "discount rate" of the co-op management plays in our parable.) To prevent members from abusing this privilege, however, the management would probably need to impose some penalty—requiring borrowers to repay more coupons than they borrowed.

Under this new system, couples would hold smaller reserves of coupons than before, knowing that they could borrow more if necessary. The co-op's officers would, however, have acquired a new tool of management. If members of the co-op reported that it was easy to find baby-sitters, hard to find opportunities to baby-sit, the terms under which members could borrow coupons could be made more favorable, encouraging more people to go out. If baby-sitters were scarce, those terms could be worsened, encouraging people to go out less.

In other words, this more sophisticated co-op would have a central bank that could stimulate a depressed economy by reducing the interest rate, cool off an overheated one by raising it.

But in Japan interest rates have fallen almost to zero, and still the economy slumps. Have we finally exhausted the usefulness of our parable?

Well, imagine that there is a seasonality in the demand and supply for baby-sitting. During the winter, when it's cold and dark, couples don't want to go out much, but are quite willing to stay home and look after other people's children—thereby accumulating points they can use on balmy summer evenings. If this seasonality isn't too pronounced, the co-op could still keep the supply and demand for baby-sitting in balance by charging low interest rates in the winter months, higher rates in the summer. But suppose that the seasonality is very strong indeed. Then in the winter, even at a zero interest rate, there will be more couples seeking opportunities to baby-sit than there are couples going out; which means that baby-sitting opportunities will be hard to find; which means that couples seeking to build up reserves for summer fun will be even less willing to use those points in the winter, meaning even fewer opportunities to baby-sit . . . and the co-op will slide into a recession even at a zero interest rate.

And now is the winter of Japan's discontent. Perhaps because of its aging population, perhaps also because of a general nervousness about the future, the Japanese public does not appear willing to spend enough to use the economy's capacity, even at a zero interest rate. Japan, say the economists, has fallen into the dread "liquidity trap"; well, what you have just read is an infantile explanation of what a liquidity trap is and how it can happen. And once you understand that this is what has gone wrong, the answer to Japan's problems is quite obvious.

Well, maybe not so obvious. Indeed, at the time of writing, Japan's authorities seemed utterly at a loss.

Japan Adrift

The standard response to a recession is to cut interest rates—to allow people to borrow baby-sitting coupons cheaply, so that they will begin going out again. Japan was a bit slow about cutting interest rates after the bubble burst, but it eventually cut them all the way to zero, and it still wasn't enough. Now what?

The classic answer, the one that has been associated with the name of John Maynard Keynes, is that if the private sector won't spend enough to maintain full employment, the public sector must take up the slack. Let the government borrow money and use the funds to finance public investment projects—if possible to good purpose, but that is a secondary consideration—and thereby provide jobs, which will make people more willing to spend, which will generate still more jobs, and so on. The Great Depression in the United States was brought to an end by a massive deficit-financed public works program, known as World War II; why not try to jump-start Japanese growth with a more pacific version of the same?

And in fact Japan tried. Since the early 1990s the government has produced a series of stimulus packages, borrowing money to build roads and bridges whether the country needed them or not. These packages created jobs directly; they also clearly did provide the economy as a whole with some boost every time they were tried.

The trouble was that the programs didn't seem to get enough bang for the yen. In 1991 Japan's government was running a fairly hefty budget surplus (2.9 percent of GDP); by 1996 it was running a quite nasty deficit of 4.3 percent of GDP. Yet the economic engine was still sputtering. Meanwhile, the ever-growing deficits were starting to worry Japan's Ministry of Finance, which was concerned about the long-term budget position. The problem was demographics (which may also have a lot to do with Japan's high savings and low investment demand). Like other countries, Japan had a baby boom followed by a baby bust, and now faces the prospect of a steadily aging population. But Japan's problem is extreme: its working-age population is actually declining steadily, even as the number of retirees rapidly grows. And since retired citizens are a heavy fiscal burden on modern governments—recipients of expensive public pensions and health care—standard fiscal principles said that Japan should be building up a trust fund now to meet the future bills, not running ever-growing deficits.

In 1997 the voices of fiscal responsibility prevailed, and Prime Minister Ryutaro Hashimoto increased taxes to reduce the budget deficit. The economy promptly plunged into recession.

So it was back to deficit spending. In 1998 Japan introduced a massive new program of public works. But the fiscal issue had now been raised, and it refused to go away. Investors soon noticed that Japan was projecting a deficit of 10 percent of GDP, and that the ratio of government debt to GDP was already above 100 percent; these are the kinds of numbers usually associated with Latin American nations at risk of hyperinflation. Nobody really expects that to happen to Japan; but in November Moody's slightly downgraded Japanese government debt, and in December the yield on Japanese government debt rose sharply, suggesting that investors were getting at least a bit worried about the long-term soundness of that government's finances. In short, the attempt to jump-start the economy with deficit spending has reached its limits.

So now what?

If government spending is one standard response to a stalled economy, pumping up the banks is another. One widely held view about the Great Depression is that it persisted so long because the banking crises of 1930–31 inflicted long-term damage to credit markets. According to this view, there were businessmen who would have been willing to spend more if they could have gotten access to credit, and who would in fact have been qualified borrowers. But the bankers who could have made those loans were themselves either out of business or unable to raise funds, because the public's confidence in banks had been so shaken. In terms of the baby-sitting co-op, this amounts to saying that there were people who would have been willing to go out in the winter and baby-sit in the summer, but who could not get anybody to lend them the necessary coupons.

Now, Japan's banks made a lot of bad loans in the bubble economy years, and the long stagnation that followed turned many other loans bad as well. For the most part the banks still have not, at the time of writing, made any realistic acknowledgment of how many of their loans will never be repaid, but everyone knows that many banks either have no capital or, at any rate, have far less than the amounts supposedly required by law. So one theory of Japan's slump is that the country is in a liquidity trap only because its banks are financially weak; fix the banks and the economy will recover. And in late 1998 Japan's legislature put together a $500 billion bank rescue plan.

The trouble is that there is little evidence that there are good loans that banks should be making but aren't. Japan has not (yet?) suffered from the kind of bank run that occurred in the United States in 1930–31, Argentina in 1995, or smaller Asian countries in the last two years. Japan's banks are still very much in existence; depositors have continued to put their money into banks, sure that the government will protect them. Indeed, the financial weakness of the banks—which means that the owners have little or no money of their own at stake—should if anything mean that the banks have an incentive to take too many risks, not too few.

True, reports of a credit crunch became widespread in late 1997—largely, it seems, because Japanese regulators were starting to become a bit more serious about enforcing the rules on bank capitalization. This credit crunch certainly contributed to the decline of more than 2 percent in Japanese output over the course of the next year. But had credit gotten tighter because banks had stopped making good loans, or because they had stopped making bad loans? Many observers suggested the latter, in which case recapitalizing the banks would not increase lending at all. In any case, the idea that bank cleanup would transform Japan's economic prospects, that it would reverse an eight-year stagnation, was a thin reed on which to rest hopes of recovery.

So was there no answer to Japan's plight?

The Inflation Heresy

The truth is that economists have not thought hard about the subject of liquidity traps for a very long time. The last time a major economy appeared to be in such a trap was the United States in the late 1930s, and historians of the period have tended to believe either that it wasn't a true liquidity trap—that the Fed could have gotten us out if it had tried hard enough—or that we got into that trap only through extraordinary policy mistakes, unlikely to be repeated. So as the outlines of Japan's trap became clear in the mid-1990s, economists were basically unprepared—and, if I may be critical of my profession, uninterested. I continue to be astonished at how few economists around the world have realized just how important a problem Japan's trap is both as a practical matter and as a challenge to our economic doctrines.

But economics is, as the great Victorian economist Alfred Marshall said, "not a body of concrete truth, but an engine for the discovery of concrete truth." Or to put it in less elevated language, old models can be taught to perform new tricks. As we saw in my revised version of the baby-sitting story, a model designed to explain why a central bank can normally cure a recession by cutting interest rates can also illuminate the circumstances under which this over-the-counter remedy does not work. And this revised parable also, it turns out, offers clear guidance on how Japan should get out of its trap.

Remember, the basic problem with the winter co-op is that people want to save the credit they earn from baby-sitting in the winter to use in the summer, even at a zero interest rate. But in the aggregate the co-op's members *can't* save up winter baby-sitting for summer use; so individual efforts to do so end up producing nothing but a winter slump.

The answer, as any economist should immediately realize, is to get the price right: to make it clear that points earned in the winter will be devalued if held until the summer—say, to make five hours of baby-sitting credit earned in the winter melt into only four hours by summer. This will encourage people to use their baby-sitting hours sooner, and hence create more baby-sitting opportunities. You might be tempted to think that there is something unfair about this—that it means expropriating people's savings. But the reality is that the co-op as a whole *cannot* bank winter baby-sitting for summer use, so it is actually distorting members' incentives to allow them to trade winter for summer hours on a one-for-one basis.

But what in the non-baby-sitting economy corresponds to our coupons that melt in the summer? The answer is that an economy which is in a liquidity trap needs expected inflation— that is, it needs to convince people that the yen they are tempted to hoard will buy less a month or a year from now than they do today.

The conclusion that what Japan really needs is a commitment to inflation is a straightforward implication of the generally accepted view that the country is indeed in a liquidity trap. I have explained that view in terms of the whimsical parable of the baby-sitting co-op, but it also pops out from application of any of the standard mathematical models that economists conventionally use to discuss monetary policy. Indeed, there has long been a strand of thought that says that moderate inflation may be necessary if monetary policy is to be able to fight recessions; one notable exponent of this view, in his pre-government days, was Deputy Treasury Secretary Lawrence Summers. It is therefore in a way surprising that no prominent economist made a forceful case for "managed inflation" in Japan until May 1998, when I circulated a short analytical piece entitled "Japan's Trap." But the often vitriolic response of both Japanese officials and Western pundits as I and a few others have made that case perhaps suggests why it took so long for anyone to make this fairly obvious point.

For it turns out that advocates of inflation have had to contend with a deep-seated sense that stable prices are always desirable, that to promote inflation is to create perverse and dangerous incentives. This belief in the importance of price stability is not based on standard economic models—on the contrary, the usual textbook theory, when applied to Japan's unusual circumstances, points directly to inflation as the natural solution. But conventional economic theory and conventional economic wisdom are not always the same thing—a conflict that would become increasingly apparent as one country after another found itself having to make hard choices in the face of financial crisis.

At the time this book was written, a heated debate was going on both inside and outside Japan about how to resolve the country's crisis. Some Japanese officials were adamant about staying with conventional policies, insisting that the economy was on the verge of recovery. But there was a minority point of view calling for "quantitative easing"—printing enough money to generate expectations of mild inflation. Pretty clearly the quantitative easers were being influenced by views of outsiders, myself included. Equally clearly, they did not expect to carry the day on policy just yet—but were publicizing their views in order to prepare the ground for a policy shift when, as they expected, further bad news finally made the time ripe for radical action.

A Note on the Yen

The baby-sitting-co-op parable is a story about a "closed" economy, one that does not trade with or invest in other economies. Opposition to the implications of that parable, on both conceptual and practical grounds, has tended to focus on Japan's relations with the rest of the world, on the idea that international trade and investment change everything. They don't; but it takes a moment to explain why.

A good placc to start is with an objection raised by *The Economist* to proposals for "managed inflation." Such a program, the magazine claimed, would not stimulate Japanese spending, because it would simply cause Japanese residents to "plonk" their savings overseas. Was the article's author right?

Well, it is surely true that expectations of inflation in Japan would make overseas investments more attractive to the Japanese public (just as lower interest rates do under normal circumstances). So other things being the same, they would indeed try to put more of their funds outside Japan. However, remember the discussion of the balance of payments in Chapter 3: the balance of payments always balances, so if Japan is going to export more capital (run a larger capital account deficit) it must also run a larger trade (strictly speaking, current account) surplus. How would this come about? If Japanese residents are trying to move their money abroad, they will be trying to convert yen into dollars, euros, etc. That will depress the value of the yen, making Japanese exports cheaper to foreigners and foreign goods more expensive to Japanese, and thereby leading to a larger trade surplus. And the yen must, as a matter of sheer accounting, fall enough to match that trade surplus to the desired export of capital.

But a bigger trade surplus means a larger demand for Japanese goods—which would help, not hurt, the economy's efforts to recover. Or to put it a bit differently, plonking would be exactly what the doctor ordered.

Now, you might wonder, in that case, how Japan can be stuck in a liquidity trap in the first place. Maybe there are not enough investments worth making in Japan, even at a zero interest rate; but aren't there plenty of investments elsewhere, say, in the United States? Why can't Japan simply export its excess savings?

The answer lies in the role of the exchange rate in the story. Suppose that Japan has a very weak yen today, allowing it to run very large trade surpluses and hence export a lot of capital. Eventually those overseas investments will mean that Japanese residents, like British investors circa 1910, receive a great deal of income from abroad—income that they will want to convert back into yen so they can spend it at home. Also, Japan will not *always* have an excess of savings over investment opportunities; as its population reaches retirement age, it will begin to draw on its savings, which will mean that overseas assets will be sold and converted back into yen. So while the yen may be weak now, this very weakness means that it will be strong in the future. And that in turn means that investing overseas is not that attractive, after all: the return measured in dollars or euros may look attractive, but if those currencies are expected to fall against the yen, the return in yen will be less—perhaps even negative. Turning this around, we can say that the fall in the yen—and hence Japan's ability to export its excess savings—will be limited by the expectation that the currency will eventually strengthen again.

So we can say that the reason Japan can be stuck in its trap, despite the ability to invest abroad, is that it *cannot get the yen weak enough*, even by reducing interest rates to zero.

Now, suppose that Japan were to accept the inflation heresy, and convince investors that prices will actually rise 3 or 4 percent per year over an extended period. This inflation would stimulate domestic demand, by making saving less attractive and borrowing more so; but it would also operate by further weakening the yen, and hence making Japanese goods more competitive on world markets. So a proposal for managed inflation is also a proposal to allow, indeed promote, a weaker yen. And that is the source of two sorts of objections—some respectable, some not.

The respectable objection is that a weakened yen could cause problems for other countries. It probably would *not* mean a much larger overall Japanese trade surplus: Japanese exports would increase, but so would Japanese imports, because consumers and investors would be spending more on goods in general. But particular countries—including, alas, the troubled smaller Asian economies, and also China—would find that a weakened yen made their lives more difficult. And particular industries in the West, notably steel, blanch at the thought of a weaker yen. These are real problems. However, an attempt to defend free capital markets and free trade by denying the world's second-largest economy the right to pursue its best hope for recovery—indeed, to insist that in this case, and only in this case, prices are not going to be allowed to match supply and demand—is surely doomed to failure.

The nonrespectable objection is that of Japanese officials who do not like the idea of having a weak currency, either because they take pride in a strong yen or because they still dream of promoting the yen as a global currency (which it may well become—but so what? The benefits to the United States of the dollar's international role are, though no one will believe it, on the order of 0.1 or 0.2 percent of GDP). Such officials remain powerful in Japan, but one hopes not for long: it would truly be tragic to see the economic interests of a great nation sacrificed on behalf of their vanity.

F I V E

■

All Fall Down:
Asia's Crash

THAILAND isn't really a small country. It has more citizens than Britain or France; Bangkok is a vast urban nightmare, whose traffic is every bit as bad as legend has it. Still, the world economy is almost inconceivably huge, and in the commercial scheme of things Thailand is pretty marginal. Despite the rapid growth of recent decades, it is still a poor country; all those people have a combined purchasing power no greater than that of the population of Massachusetts. One might have thought that Thai economic affairs, unlike those of an economic behemoth like Japan, were of interest only to the Thais, their immediate neighbors, and those businesses with a direct financial stake in the country.

But the 1997 devaluation of Thailand's currency, the baht, triggered a financial avalanche that buried much of Asia. The crucial questions are why that happened and, indeed, how it even *could* have happened. But before we get to why and how, let's review what: the story of Thailand's boom, its crash, and the spread of that crash across Asia.

The Boom

Thailand was a relative latecomer to the Asian miracle. Traditionally mainly an agricultural exporter, it started to become a major industrial center only in the 1980s, when foreign firms—especially Japanese—began siting plants in the country. But when the economy did take off, it did so very impressively: as peasants moved from the countryside into the new urban jobs, as the good results experienced by the first wave of foreign investors encouraged others to follow, Thailand began growing at 8 percent or more per year. Soon the famed temples of Bangkok lay in the shadow of office and apartment towers; like its neighbors, Thailand became a place where millions of ordinary people were beginning to emerge from desperate poverty into at least the beginnings of a decent life, and where some people were becoming very rich.

Until the early 1990s, most of the investment associated with this growth came from the savings of the Thais themselves: foreign money built the big export factories, but the smaller businesses were financed by local businessmen out of their own savings; the new office and apartment blocks were financed out of the bank deposits of domestic households. In 1991 Thailand's foreign debt was slightly less than its annual exports—not a trivial ratio, but one that was well within normal bounds of safety. (In the same year Latin American debt averaged 2.7 times exports.)

During the 1990s, however, this financial self-sufficiency began to change. Mainly the push came from outside. The resolution of the Latin debt crisis, described in Chapter 3, made investment in the Third World respectable again. The fall of Communism, by diminishing the perceived threat of radical takeover, made investing outside the safety of the Western world seem less risky than before. In the early 1990s interest rates in advanced countries were exceptionally low, because central banks were trying to boot their economies out of a mild recession; many investors went abroad in search of higher yields. Perhaps most crucial of all, investment funds coined a new name for what had previously been called Third World or developing countries: now they were "emerging markets," the new frontier of financial opportunity.

Investors responded in droves. In 1990 private capital flows to developing countries were $42 billion; official agencies like the IMF and the World Bank were actually financing more investment in the Third World than all private investors combined. By 1997, however, while the flow of official money had actually slowed, private flows had quintupled, to $256 billion. At first most of the money went to Latin America, especially Mexico; but after 1994 it increasingly went to the apparently safer economies of Southeast Asia.

How did the money get from Tokyo or Frankfurt (most of the lending to Asia was Japanese or European—through wisdom or luck, U.S. banks mainly stayed on the sidelines) to Bangkok or Djakarta? What did it do when it got there? Let's follow the steps.

Start with a typical transaction: a Japanese bank makes a loan to a Thai "finance company," an institution whose main purpose is to act as a conveyor belt for foreign funds. The finance company now has yen, which it uses to make a loan at a higher interest rate, to a local real estate developer. But the developer wants to borrow baht, not yen, since he must buy land and pay his workers in local currency. So the finance company goes to the foreign exchange market and exchanges its yen for baht.

Now, the foreign exchange market, like other markets, is governed by the law of supply and demand: increase the demand for something, and its price will normally rise. That is, the demand for baht by the finance company will tend to make the baht rise in value against other currencies. But during the boom years Thailand's central bank was committed to maintaining a stable rate of exchange between the baht and the U.S. dollar. To do this, it would have to offset any increase in the demand for baht by also increasing the supply: selling baht and buying foreign currencies like the dollar or yen. So the indirect result of that initial yen loan would be an increase both in the Bank of Thailand's reserves of foreign exchange and in the Thai money supply. And there would also be an expansion of credit in the economy—not only the loan directly provided by the finance company but additional credit provided by the banks in which the newly created baht were deposited; and since much of the money lent out would itself end up back in the banks in the form of new deposits, this would finance yet further new loans, and so on, in the classic "money multiplier" process taught in Econ 101. (My description of Argentina's 1995 banking crisis was an example of this same process running in reverse.)

As more and more loans poured in from abroad, then, the result was a massive expansion of credit, which fueled a wave of new investment. Some of this took the form of actual construction, mainly office and apartment buildings, but there was also a lot of pure speculation, mainly in real estate, but also in stocks. By early 1996 the economies of Southeast Asia were starting to bear a strong family resemblance to Japan's "bubble economy" of the late 1980s.

Why didn't the monetary authorities put curbs on the speculative boom? The answer is that they tried, but failed. In all the Asian economies, central banks tried to "sterilize" the capital inflows: obliged to sell baht in the foreign exchange market, the Bank of Thailand would try to buy those baht back elsewhere by selling bonds, in effect borrowing back the money it had just printed. But this borrowing drove up local interest rates, making borrowing from overseas even more attractive and pulling in yet more yen and dollars. The effort to sterilize failed: credit just kept on growing.

The only way the central bank could have prevented money and credit from ballooning would have been to stop trying to fix the exchange rate—to have simply let the baht rise. And this is indeed what many Monday-morning quarterbacks now say the Thais should have done. But at the time this seemed like a bad idea: a stronger baht would make Thai exports less competitive on world markets (because wages and other costs would be higher in dollars), and in general the Thais thought that a stable exchange rate was good for business confidence, that they

were too small a nation to endure the kind of widely fluctuat-
ing exchange rate the United States can live with.

And so the boom was allowed to run its course. Eventually,
as the textbook would tell you, the expansion of money and
credit was self-limiting. Soaring investment, together with a
surge of spending by newly affluent consumers, led to a surge
in imports; the booming economy pulled up wages, making
Thai exports less competitive (especially because China, an
important competitor for Thailand, had devalued its own currency in 1994), so export growth slowed down. The result was
a huge trade deficit; instead of feeding domestic money and
credit, those foreign-currency loans started paying for imports.

And why not? Some economists argued—just as Mexico's
boosters had argued in the early 1990s—that the trade deficits
of Thailand, Malaysia, and Indonesia were a sign not of economic weakness but of economic strength, of markets working
the way they were supposed to. To repeat the argument: as a
matter of sheer accounting, a country that is attracting net
inflows of capital must be running a current account deficit of
equal size. So as long as you thought that the capital inflows to
Southeast Asia were economically justified, so were the trade
deficits. And why wasn't it reasonable for the world to invest a
lot of capital in Southeast Asia, given the region's record of
growth and economic stability? After all, this wasn't a case of
governments on a spending spree: while Malaysia and Indonesia had their share of grandiose public projects, they were being
paid for out of current revenue, and budgets were more or less
in balance. So these trade deficits were the product of private-
sector decisions; why should these decisions be second-
guessed?

Still, a growing number of observers started to feel a bit
uneasy as the deficits of Thailand and Malaysia grew to 6, 7, 8
percent of GDP—the sorts of numbers Mexico had had before
the tequila crisis. The Mexican experience had convinced
some of us that international capital flows, even if they represented the undistorted decisions of the private sector, were not
necessarily to be trusted; the bullishness of investors about

Asian prospects bore a disturbing resemblance to their bullishness about Latin America a couple of years earlier. And the Mexican experience also suggested that a reversal of market sentiment, when it came, would be sharp and hard to deal with.

What we also should have noticed was that the claim that Asian borrowing represented free private-sector decisions was not quite the truth. For Southeast Asia, like Japan in the bubble years, had a moral hazard problem—the problem that would soon be dubbed crony capitalism.

Let's go back to that Thai finance company, the institution that borrowed the yen that started the whole process of credit expansion. What, exactly, were these finance companies? They were not, as it happens, ordinary banks: by and large they had few if any depositors. Nor were they like Western investment banks, repositories of specialized information that could help direct funds to their most profitable uses. So what was their reason for existence? What did they bring to the table?

The answer, basically, was political connections—often, indeed, the owner of the finance company was a relative of some government official. And so the claim that the decisions about how much to borrow and invest represented private-sector judgments, not to be second-guessed, rang more than a bit hollow. True, loans to finance companies were not subject to the kind of formal guarantees that backed deposits in U.S. savings and loans. But foreign banks that lent money to the minister's nephew's finance company can be forgiven for believing that they had a little extra protection, that the minister would find a way to rescue the company if its investments did not work out as planned. And the foreign lenders would have been right: in roughly nine out of ten cases, foreign lenders to finance companies did indeed get bailed out by the Thai government when the crisis came.

Now look at the situation from the point of view of the minister's nephew, the owner of the finance company. Basically, he was in a position to borrow money at low rates, no questions asked. What, then, could be more natural than to lend that money at a high rate of interest to his friend the real estate developer, whose speculative new office tower just might make a killing—but then again might not. If all went well, fine: both men would have made a lot of money. If things did not turn out as hoped, well, not so terrible: the minister would find a way to save the finance company. Heads the nephew wins, tails the taxpayer loses.

One way or another, similar games were being played in all the countries that would soon be caught up in the crisis. In Indonesia middlemen played less of a role: there the typical dubious transaction was a direct loan from a foreign bank to a company controlled by one of the president's cronies. (The quintessential example was the loan that broke Hong Kong's Peregrine Investment Holdings, a loan made directly to Suharto's daughter's taxi company.) In Korea the big borrowers were banks effectively controlled by *chaebol*, the huge conglomerates that have dominated the nation's economy and—until very recently—its politics. Throughout the region, then, implicit government guarantees were helping underwrite investments that were both riskier and less promising than would have been undertaken without those guarantees, adding fuel to what would probably anyway have been an overheated speculative boom.

Given all of this, the development of some kind of crisis was not too surprising. Some of us can even claim to have predicted currency crises more than a year in advance. But nobody realized just how severe the crisis would be.

July 2

During 1996 and the first half of 1997 the credit machine that had created Thailand's boom began to slip into reverse. Partly this was because of external events: markets for some of Thailand's exports went soft, a depreciation of Japan's yen made Southeast Asian industry a bit less competitive. Mostly, though, it was simply a matter of the house beating the gamblers, which in the long run it always does: a growing number of the speculative investments that had been financed, directly or indirectly, by cheap foreign loans went sour. Some speculators went bust; some finance companies went out of business. And foreign lenders became increasingly reluctant to lend any more money.

This was to a certain extent a self-reinforcing process. As long as real estate prices and stock markets were booming, even questionable investments tended to look good. As the air began to go out of the bubble, losses began to mount, further reducing confidence and causing the supply of fresh loans to shrink even more. Even before the July 2 crisis, land and stocks had fallen a long way from their peaks.

The slowdown in foreign borrowing also posed problems for the central bank. With fewer yen and dollars coming in, the demand for baht on the foreign exchange market declined; meanwhile, the need to change baht into foreign currencies to pay for imports continued unabated. In order to keep the value of the baht from declining, the Bank of Thailand therefore had to do the opposite of what it had done when capital starting coming in: it came into the market to exchange dollars and yen for baht, supporting its own currency. But there is an important difference between trying to keep your currency down and trying to keep it up: the Bank of Thailand can increase the supply of baht as much as it likes, because it can simply print them; but it cannot print dollars. So there was a limit on its ability to keep the baht up: sooner or later it would run out of reserves.

The only way to sustain the value of the currency would have been to reduce the number of baht in circulation, driving up interest rates and thus making it attractive once again to borrow dollars to reinvest in baht. But this posed problems of a different sort. As the investment boom sputtered out, the Thai economy had slowed—there was less construction activity, which meant fewer jobs, which meant lower income, which meant layoffs in the rest of the economy—not quite a full-fledged recession, but still the economy was no longer living in the style to which it had become accustomed. To raise interest rates would be to discourage investment further, and perhaps push the economy into an unambiguous slump.

The alternative was to let the currency go: to stop buying baht, and let the exchange rate slide. But this too was an awkward answer, not only because such a devaluation of the currency would hurt the government's reputation but because so many banks, finance companies, and other Thai businesses now had debts in dollars; if the value of the dollar in terms of baht were to increase, many of them would find themselves insolvent.

And so the Thai government dithered. It was not willing to let the baht fall; nor was it willing to take the kind of harsh domestic measures that would have stemmed the loss in reserves. Instead, it played a waiting game, apparently hoping that something would eventually turn up.

All of this was according to the standard script: it was the classic lead-in to a currency crisis, of the kind that economists love to model—and speculators love to provoke. As it became clear that the government did not have the stomach to turn the screws on the domestic economy, it became increasingly likely that eventually the baht would be allowed to fall in value. But since it hadn't happened yet, there was still time to take advantage of the prospective event. As long as the baht-dollar exchange rate seemed likely to remain stable, the fact that interest rates in Thailand were several points higher than in the United States provided an incentive to borrow in dollars, and lend in baht. But once it became a high probability that the baht would soon be devalued, the incentive was to go the other way—to borrow in baht, expecting that the dollar value of these debts would soon be reduced, and acquire dollars, expecting that the baht value of these assets would soon increase. Local businessmen borrowed in baht and paid off their dollar loans; wealthy Thais sold their holdings of government debt and bought U.S. Treasury bills; and last but not least, some large international hedge funds began borrowing baht and converting the proceeds into dollars.

All of these actions involved selling baht and buying other currencies; which meant that they all required the central bank to buy even more baht to keep the currency from falling, and depleted its reserves of foreign exchange even faster—which further reinforced the conviction that the baht was going to be devalued sooner rather than later. A classic currency crisis was in full swing.

Any money doctor can tell you that once things have reached that point the government must move decisively, one way or the other: either make a clear commitment to defend the currency at all costs, or let it go. But governments usually have a hard time making either decision. Like many governments before and no doubt many to come, Thailand's waited as its reserves ran down; trying to convince markets that its position was stronger than it was, it made those reserves look larger through unannounced "currency swaps" (in effect, borrowing dollars now for repayment later). But though the pressure sometimes seemed to abate, it always resumed. By the beginning of July, it was clear that the game was up. On July 2, the Thais let the baht go.

Up to this point, nothing all that surprising had happened. The rundown of reserves, the speculative attack on an obviously weak currency, were right out of the textbooks. But despite the recent experience of the tequila crisis, most people thought that the devaluation of the baht would pretty much end the story: a humiliation for the government, perhaps a nasty shock for some overstretched businesses, but nothing catastrophic. Surely Thailand looked nothing like Mexico. Nobody could accuse it of having achieved "stabilization, reform, and no growth"; there was no Thai Cárdenas, waiting in the wings to enforce a populist program. And so there would not be a devastating recession.

We were wrong.

Meltdown

There are two somewhat different questions to ask about the recession that spread across Asia in the wake of the Thai devaluation. The first is one of mechanics: how did this slump happen? Why should a devaluation in one small economy have provoked a collapse of investment and output across so wide an area? The other, in a way deeper, question is why governments did not, perhaps could not, prevent the catastrophe. What happened to macroeconomic policy?

That second question will take some time to answer, at least partly because it is a matter of very sharp disagreement among reasonable people. So let's leave it until the next chapter, and simply try to describe what happened.

When all goes well, nothing terrible happens when a currency is allowed to drop in value. When Britain abandoned its defense of the pound in 1992, the currency dropped about 15 percent, then stabilized: investors figured that the worst was over, that the lower currency would help the country's exports, and that it was therefore a better place to invest than it had been before. Typical calculations suggested that the baht would have to fall something like 15 percent to make Thai industry cost-competitive again, so a decline of roughly that magnitude seemed likely. But instead, the currency went into free fall: the baht price of a dollar soared 50 percent over the next few months, and would have risen even further if Thailand had not sharply raised interest rates.

Why did the baht fall so far? The short answer is "panic"; but there are panics and panics. Which was it?

Sometimes a panic is just a panic: an irrational reaction on the part of investors that is not justified by the actual news. An example might be the brief plunge in the dollar in 1981, after a deranged gunman wounded Ronald Reagan. It was a shocking event; but even if Reagan had died, the stability of the U.S. government and the continuity of its policy could hardly have been affected. Those who kept their heads and did not flee the dollar were rewarded for their cool heads.

Much more important in economics, however, are panics that, whatever sets them off, validate themselves—because the panic itself makes panic justified. The classic example is a bank run: when all of a bank's depositors try to withdraw their money at once, the bank is forced to sell its assets at distress prices, causing it to go bankrupt; those depositors who did not panic end up worse off than those who did.

And indeed there *were* some bank runs in Thailand, and even more in Indonesia. But to focus only on these bank runs would be to take the metaphor too literally. What really happened was a circular process—a devastating feedback loop—of financial deterioration and declining confidence, of which conventional bank runs were only one aspect.

The accompanying figure illustrates this process, which occurred in some version in all of the afflicted Asian economies, schematically. Start anywhere in the circle—say, with a decline of confidence in Thailand's currency and economy. This decline in confidence would make investors, both domestic and foreign, want to pull their money out of the country. Other things being the same, this would cause the baht to plunge in value. Since the Thai central bank could no longer support the value of its currency by buying it on the foreign exchange market (because it no longer had dollars or yen to spend), the only way it could limit the currency's decline was to raise interest rates and pull baht out of circulation. Unfortunately, both the decline in the currency's value and the rise in interest rates created financial problems for businesses, both financial institutions and other companies. On one side, many of them had dollar debts, which suddenly became more burdensome as the number of baht per dollar increased; on the other, many of them also had baht debts,

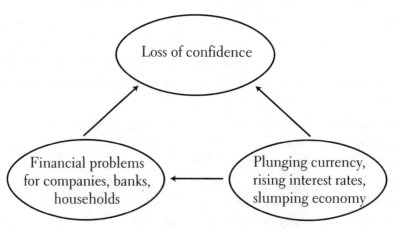

The Vicious Circle of Financial Crisis

which became harder to service as interest rates soared. And the combination of higher interest rates and troubled balance sheets with a banking system that often found itself unable to make even the safest of loans meant that companies had to slash spending, causing a recession, which in turn meant still worse news for profits and balance sheets. All this bad news from the economy, inevitably, reduced confidence still further—and the economy went into a meltdown.

Leaving aside all the complicated details (which are still being picked over by researchers), this story seems fairly straightforward—especially because something quite similar happened in Mexico in 1995. So why did the disastrous effects of Thailand's devaluation come as such a surprise? The basic answer is that while many economists were aware of the elements of this story—everyone understood that the feedback from confidence, to financial markets, to the real economy, and back again to confidence existed in principle—nobody realized just how powerful that feedback process would be in practice. And as a result nobody realized how explosive the circular logic of crisis could be.

Here's a parallel. A microphone in an auditorium always generates a feedback loop: sounds picked up by the microphone are amplified by the loudspeakers; the output from the speakers is itself picked up by the microphone; and so on. But as long as the room isn't too echoey and the gain isn't too high, this is a "damped" process, and poses no problem. Turn the dial a little too far to the right, however, and the process becomes explosive: any little sound is picked up, amplified, picked up again, and suddenly there is an earsplitting screech. What matters, in other words, is not just the qualitative fact of feedback, but its quantitative strength; what caught everyone by surprise was the discovery that the dial was in fact turned up so high.

Indeed, even now there are many people who find it hard to believe that a market economy can really be that unstable, that the feedbacks illustrated in the figure can really be strong enough to create an explosive crisis. But they are—as we can see by looking at the way the crisis spread.

Contagion

There is probably a good reason why important meetings about international finance, especially about international crisis management, tend to take place in rustic resorts—why the postwar monetary system was hammered out at the Mount Washington Hotel at Bretton Woods, why many of the world's finance ministers and central bankers gather each summer at Jackson Lake Lodge in Wyoming. Perhaps the setting helps important people get away from the firefighting of their daily lives, and focus at least briefly on the larger issues. In any case, in early October 1997—when the Asian crisis was well underway, but its severity was not yet clear—a number of bankers, officials, and economists converged on Woodstock, Vermont, to take stock.

By then Thailand was already pretty clearly in deep trouble; the currency of its neighbor Malaysia had also been battered; and the Indonesian rupiah had depreciated about 30 percent. The general sense in the room was that Thailand had brought its woes on itself; and there was little sympathy for Malaysia, which like Thailand had been running huge current account deficits in the past several years, and whose prime minister had clearly made things worse with his denunciations of evil speculators. But everyone agreed that while Indonesia had been right to let its currency slide—indeed, many good things were said about Indonesia's economic management—the rupiah's weakness was not really justified. After all, Indonesia's current account deficits had been nowhere near as large relative to GDP as its neighbors'—at less than 4 percent of GDP, Indonesia's 1996 deficit was actually smaller than, say, Australia's. The country's export base—part raw materials, part labor-intensive manufacturing—looked solid; and in general the economy looked fundamentally sound.

Within three months Indonesia was in even worse shape than the rest of Southeast Asia, indeed on its way to one of the worst economic slumps in world history; and the crisis had spread not just across Southeast Asia but all the way to South

Korea, a faraway economy whose GDP was twice as large as that of Indonesia, three times as large as that of Thailand.

There are sometimes good reasons for economic contagion. An old line says that when the United States sneezes, Canada catches cold; no wonder, when much of Canada's production is sold in the markets of its giant southern neighbor. And there were some direct links among the afflicted Asian economies: Thailand is a market for Malaysian products and vice versa. A bit of extra traction may have been generated by the tendency of the Asian economies to sell similar products to third parties: when Thailand devalued its currency, the clothing it exports to the West got cheaper, and therefore cut into the profit margins of Indonesian producers of similar items.

But all estimates of this direct, "goods market" spillover among the crisis economies indicate that it just can't have been a major factor in the spread of the crisis. In particular, Thailand's role either as a market for or competitor of South Korea was little more than rounding error for the far larger Korean economy.

A more potent source of contagion may have been more or less direct financial linkage. Not that Thais were big investors in Korea, or Koreans in Thailand; but the flows of money into the region were often channeled through "emerging market funds" that lumped all the countries together. When bad news came in from Thailand, money flowed out of these funds, and hence out of all the countries in the region.

Even more important than this mechanical linkage, however, was the way that Asian economies were associated in the minds of investors. The appetite of investors for the region had been fed by the perception of a shared "Asian miracle"; when one country's economy turned out not to be all that miraculous after all, it shook faith in all the others. The wise men at Woodstock may have regarded Indonesia as quite different from Thailand, but the investor in the street was less sure and began to pull back just in case.

And it turned out that whatever the differences among all those economies, one thing they did have in common was susceptibility to self-validating panic. The wise men at Woodstock were wrong about Indonesia, and the panicky investors right; this was not because the wise men had misjudged Indonesia's virtues but because they had underestimated its vulnerability. In Malaysia, in Indonesia, in Korea, as in Thailand, the market's loss of confidence started a vicious circle of financial and economic collapse. It did not matter that these economies were only modestly linked in terms of physical flows of goods. They were linked in the minds of investors, who regarded the troubles of one Asian economy as bad news about the others; and when an economy is vulnerable to self-validating panic, believing makes it so.

Why Asia? Why 1997?

Why did Asia experience a terrible economic crisis, and why did it begin in 1997? As Bill Clinton might put it, the answer depends on what you mean by "why." You might be asking about the specific precipitating events; or you might, more important, be asking about the source of Asia's extraordinary vulnerability.

If you insist on placing the blame for the onset of the Asian crisis on some specific event, there is a list of usual suspects. One is the exchange rate between the yen and the dollar: between 1995 and 1997 the yen, which had rather mysteriously gone to sky-high levels, fell back to earth. Since most Asian currencies were more or less pegged to the dollar, this made their exports look more expensive both in Japanese markets and in competition with Japanese products elsewhere, contributing to an export slowdown. China's 1994 devaluation, and more broadly growing competition from China's cheap labor, likewise cut into Thai and Malaysian exports. And there was a worldwide slump in the demand for electronics in general and semiconductors in particular, an area in which Asia's economies had tended to specialize.

But Asia had shrugged off much bigger shocks before. The 1985 crash in oil prices, for example, was a major blow to oil-exporting Indonesia; yet the economy grew right through the bad news. The 1990–91 recession, which was not very severe but affected much of the industrial world, reduced the demand for Asia's exports but did not slow the region's momentum at all. So the important question is what had changed about Asia (or perhaps the world), so that *these* pieces of bad news triggered an economic avalanche.

Some of the Asians, notably Malaysia's Prime Minister Mahathir, had a ready answer: conspiracy. Mahathir, indeed, argued not only that the panic in Asia was deliberately engineered by big financial operators like George Soros but that Soros himself was acting on instructions from the U.S. government, which wanted to cut assertive Asians down to size. As time has gone by, Mahathir's demonization of hedge funds has started to look a bit less silly than it did when he first began his ranting. Indeed, the role of hedge funds now looks important enough to rate a whole chapter in this book (Chapter 7). But that role became important mainly in 1998 (by which time, incidentally, the activities of Soros and others were very much contrary to U.S. policy wishes); as a story about how the crisis began, conspiracy theory doesn't wash.

On the other side, many Westerners have turned the story of Asia's crash into a sort of morality play, in which the economies received their inevitable punishment for the sins of crony capitalism. After the catastrophe, everyone had a story about the excesses and corruption of the region—about those finance companies, about Malaysia's grandiose plans for a "technology corridor," about the fortunes made by Suharto's family, about the bizarre diversification of Korean conglomerates (did you hear the one about the underwear company that bought a ski resort, and eventually had to sell it to Michael Jackson?). But this morality play is problematic on at least two counts.

First, while cronyism and corruption were very real in Asia, they were nothing new. Korea's *chaebol* were essentially family enterprises disguised as modern corporations, whose owners had been accustomed to special treatment—preferred access to credit, to import licenses, to government subsidies—for decades. And those were decades of spectacular economic growth. It was not a pretty system by Western standards; but it did function very well for thirty-five years. The same may be said, to a lesser extent, of all the countries caught up in the crisis. Why did their flaws become crucial only in 1997?

And a related point: if the crisis was a punishment for the sins of the Asian economies, how was it that economies that were by no means equally far down the path of development all hit the wall at the same time? Korea in 1997 was not far short of being a developed nation, with per capita income comparable to that of southern European countries; Indonesia was still a very poor country, where progress could be measured in terms of how many calories a day people managed to consume. How is it that such an ill-matched pair could simultaneously be plunged into crisis?

The only answer that makes sense to me, at least, is that the crisis was *not* (mainly) a punishment for sins. There were real failings in these economies, but the main failing was a vulnerability to self-fulfilling panic.

Back to bank runs: in 1931, about half the banks in the United States failed. These banks were not all alike. Some were very badly run; some took excessive risks, even given what they knew before 1929; others were reasonably well, even conservatively managed. But when panic spread across the land, and depositors everywhere wanted their money immediately, none of this mattered: only banks that had been extremely conservative, that had kept what in normal times would be an excessively large share of their deposits in cash, survived. Similarly, Thailand had a badly run economy, that had borrowed far too much and invested it in very dubious projects; Indonesia, for all its corruption, was much less culpable, and truly had the virtues those wise men imagined; but in the panic those distinctions did not matter.

Were the Asian economies more vulnerable to financial panic in 1997 than they had been, say, five or ten years before? Yes, surely—but not because of crony capitalism, or indeed what would usually be considered bad government policies.

Rather, they had become more vulnerable partly because they had opened up their financial markets—because they had, in fact, become better free-market economies, not worse. And they had also grown vulnerable because they had taken advantage of their new popularity with international lenders to run up substantial debts to the outside world. These debts intensified the feedback from loss of confidence to financial collapse and back again, making the vicious circle of crisis more intense. It wasn't that the money was badly spent; some of it was, some of it wasn't. It was that the new debts, unlike the old ones, were in dollars—and that turned out to be the economies' undoing.

The Deeper Question

Most commentators on the Asian crisis would probably find some detail of the account in this chapter to quarrel with. Some would argue that the damage done by moral-hazard-driven lending was greater than I suggest; some would argue, on the contrary, that the economies were really in very good shape, and that the crisis was wholly gratuitous. The precise mechanism of crisis—the respective roles of bank failures, real estate prices, exchange rates, interest rates, and so on—will be the subject of much wrangling for years, perhaps decades to come. Nonetheless, in a general sense I believe that this account would receive broad acceptance.

The real controversy—the one that is heated and often personal, because those who criticize the way the crisis was handled are also criticizing those who handled it—concerns policy. Wasn't there something that could have been done to limit the damage to Asia? Did policymakers fall down on the job? Did they, in fact, make things worse?

S I X

■

The Confidence Game

IN December 1930, just as it started to become obvious that this was no ordinary recession, John Maynard Keynes attempted to explain the causes of the slump to the general public. "We have magneto [alternator] trouble," he declared. It was, in a way, a radical statement, for he was declaring that the economic engine would not restart of its own accord, that it needed a jump start from the government. But in a deeper sense Keynes was being a conservative: he was declaring that the trouble with the engine was not fundamental, that it was amenable to a technical fix. At a time when many of the world's intellectuals were convinced that capitalism was a failed system, that only by moving to a centrally planned economy could the West emerge from the Great Depression, Keynes was saying that capitalism was *not* doomed, that a very limited sort of inter-vention—intervention that would leave private property and private decision making intact—was all that was needed to make the system work.

Confounding the skeptics, capitalism did survive; but although today's free-market enthusiasts may find this proposition hard to accept, that survival was basically on the terms Keynes suggested. World War II provided the jump start Keynes had been urging for years; but what restored faith in free markets was not just the recovery from the Depression but the assurance that macroeconomic intervention—cutting interest rates or increasing budget deficits to fight recessions—could keep a free-market economy more or less stable at more or less full employment. In effect, capitalism and its economists made a deal with the public: it will be okay to have free markets from now on, because we know enough to prevent any more Great Depressions.

This implicit deal actually has a name: in the 1950s Paul Samuelson, in his famous textbook, called it the "neoclassical synthesis." But I prefer to think of it as the "Keynesian compact."

In the United States and most other advanced countries, that compact is still honored. Oh, there are recessions now and then. However, when they occur, everyone expects the Federal Reserve to do what it did in 1975, 1982, and 1991: cut interest rates to perk up the economy. And we also expect the president and Congress to cut taxes and raise spending if necessary to help the process. We surely do not expect that a recession will be met, Herbert Hoover style, by raising taxes, cutting spending, and increasing interest rates.

But when financial disaster struck Asia, the policies those countries followed in response were almost exactly the reverse of what the United States does in the face of a slump. Fiscal austerity was the order of the day; interest rates were increased, often to punitive levels. This was not because the policymakers in those countries were stupid or ill informed. On the contrary, for the most part they understood the Keynesian compact very well, indeed had tried to adhere to it in the past (remember the World Bank's praise for their "pragmatic orthodoxy"). Anyway, once the crisis struck, Asian countries found their policies largely dictated by Washington—that is, by the International Monetary Fund and the U.S. Treasury. And the leadership of those institutions is extremely sophisticated: one could argue that never in history have so many first-rate economists been in positions of so much authority.

Why did these extremely clever men advocate policies for emerging market economies that would have been regarded as completely perverse if applied at home? (If the United States were to raise taxes and interest rates in the face of a recession, we too might experience an economic meltdown.) The short answer is "fear of speculators." But that short answer makes sense only if put in context—specifically, if we spend some time trying to understand the dilemmas of international money.

How the International Monetary System Didn't Evolve

Once upon a time, the world had a single currency, the globo. It was well managed: the Global Reserve Bank (popularly known as the Glob), under its chairman Alan Globespan, did a pretty good job of increasing the global money supply when the world threatened to slide into recession, trimming it when there were indications of inflation. Indeed, in later years some would remember the reign of the globo as a golden age. Businessmen in particular liked the system, because they could buy and sell anywhere with a minimum of hassle.

But there was trouble in paradise. You see, although careful management of the globo could prevent a boom-bust cycle *for the world as a whole*, it could not do so for each piece of that whole. Indeed, it turned out that there were often conflicts of interest about monetary policy. Sometimes the Glob would be following an easy-money policy because Europe and Asia were on the edge of recession; but that easy money would fuel a wild speculative boom in North America. At other times the Glob would feel obliged to tighten money to head off inflation in North America, intensifying a developing recession in South America. And because there were no separate continental currencies, there was nothing continental governments could do about these problems.

Eventually there came a time when the frustrations grew too great, and the system broke up. Instead of the globo, each continent introduced its own currency, and proceeded to pursue monetary policies tailored to its own needs. When Europe's economy was overheating, it could reduce the supply of euros; when Latin America slumped, it could increase the supply of latinos. The awkwardness of a one-size-fits-all monetary policy was gone.

But it soon turned out that disposing of one problem created another because the exchange rates between continental currencies fluctuated wildly. One might have thought that the exchange rate between, say, the latino and the euro would be determined by the needs of trade: by Latin Americans trading latinos for euros in order to buy European goods, and conversely. It soon became clear, however, that the market was dominated mainly by investors—people buying and selling currencies in order to purchase stocks and bonds. And since these investment demands were highly variable, including a large component of speculation, currency values also proved unstable. Worse yet, people began to speculate on the values of the currencies themselves. The result was that exchange rates bounced around, creating uncertainty for businesses, which could never be sure what their overseas assets and liabilities were really worth.

So some continents tried to stabilize exchange rates—buying and selling on the foreign exchange market in order to keep the price of a euro in terms of afros, or a gringo in terms of latinos, constant. Central banks reserved the right, however, to change the target exchange rates if necessary—say, by devaluing their currency if this seemed necessary to fight unemployment.

Alas, this "adjustable peg" system turned out to offer speculators too many easy targets: when a continent experienced economic difficulties, and started to look as if it might consider a devaluation, speculators would begin selling its currency in anticipation; this would soon force the continental central bank either to raise interest rates, actually worsening the slump, or devalue immediately. Or—the one remaining option—it could try to defeat the speculators directly, by placing restrictions on the movement of capital.

And so the world's continents were forced into choosing one

of three "currency regimes," each of which had a serious defect. They could opt to maintain an independent monetary policy and let the exchange rate fluctuate as it pleased; this left them free to fight recessions, but introduced disturbing uncertainty into business life. They could fix the value of the exchange rate and attempt to convince markets that they would never devalue; this would make business life simpler and safer, but would bring back the problem of one-size-fits-all monetary policy. Or they could continue to maintain an adjustable peg, that is, fix the exchange rate but retain the option of changing it; but this was workable only if they maintained controls on capital movement, which were hard to enforce, imposed extra costs on business, and—like any prohibition on potentially profitable transactions—were a source of corruption.

Okay, okay, it didn't really happen quite that way. There never was a globo; the closest thing to it was the pre-1930s gold standard, which unfortunately was *not* managed so as to prevent worldwide booms and busts. But our imaginary history does illustrate a bit more clearly than the complexities of what actually happened the three-cornered dilemma, or "trilemma," that national economies face in a global economy.

Think of it this way. There are three things that macroeconomic managers want for their economies. They want discretion in monetary policy, so that they can fight recessions and curb inflation. They want stable exchange rates, so that businesses are not faced with too much uncertainty. And they want to leave international business free—in particular, to allow people to exchange money however they like—in order to get out of the private sector's way.

What the story of the globo and its demise tells us is that countries cannot get all three wishes; at most, they can get two. They can give up on exchange rate stability; this means adopting a floating exchange rate, like the United States or Australia. They can give up on discretionary monetary policy; this means fixing the exchange rate, the way Argentina has, and possibly even giving up your own currency, like the nations of continental Europe. Or they can give up on the principle of com-

pletely free markets and impose capital controls; this was what
most countries did between the 1940s and the 1960s, and what
China and Malaysia do right now.

Which of these three imperfect answers is best? There are
some people who think that the gains from stable exchange
rates are large, the benefits of independent monetary policy
overrated; they like to point out that the United States, though
spread over a continent, does very well with a single currency;
some 300 million Europeans have just adopted a common currency; so why not the world as a whole? But most economists
will point out that the United States has special features that
help it live with a single currency: most notably, workers can
and do move rapidly from depressed to booming regions, so
that one size of monetary policy more or less does fit all. The
introduction of the euro, Europe's new currency, is in fact quite
controversial, with many economists questioning whether
Europe is anywhere near as suited to a single money as the
United States. But at least the major European economies are
rather similar to each other and very closely linked, so that most
of the time a monetary policy that is appropriate for France will
also be appropriate for Germany, and vice versa. It is hard to
see, however, how a suitable monetary policy could be devised
that was appropriate for both Japan and the United States, let
alone the United States and Argentina. So relatively few economists are nostalgic for the days of the gold standard, or fanta-
size about the coming of the globo; national, or perhaps
regional, monetary independence is still needed.

On the other hand, the capital controls that allowed advanced
countries to combine fixed exchange rates with Keynesian policies in the first postwar generation are now very much
out of fashion. The fundamental problem with these controls is
that the distinction between "good" and "bad" international
transactions is a hard one to make. A speculator who pulls his
money out of Malaysia because he is trying to profit from a
devaluation is engaged in an antisocial act; a Malaysian exporter
who wins customers abroad in part by letting them buy now, pay
later is helping the country earn its way in world markets. But

suppose that the exporter, suspecting that the ringgit will soon be devalued, asks his customers to pay in dollars and encourages them to take a long time before settling. The effect is the same as if he took ringgit and bought dollars on the black market. And there are dozens of other ways in which the line between productive business and currency speculation can be blurred. What this means is either that attempts to control speculation will be easily evaded or that the government can limit speculation only by imposing onerous restrictions on ordinary transactions (e.g., limiting the credit exporters can give their customers). Forty years ago most governments regarded these restrictions as a price worth paying. Today, however, we live in a world that has relearned the virtues of free markets, is suspicious of government intervention, and is particularly aware that the more things are prohibited, the greater the scope for bribery and cronyism.

Which leaves freely floating exchange rates, which by the mid-1990s most economists had come to regard as the lesser of three evils. True, exchange rates have repeatedly proved to be far more volatile than they "should" be, given economic fundamentals (over the past five years the dollar-yen rate has gone from 120, to 80, to nearly 150, then back below 110, all with relatively little measurable change in fundamentals); and even those who are generally pro-floating agree that tightly integrated regions that form "optimal currency areas" should adopt the ultimate form of fixed exchange rates, a common currency. (Whether Europe constitutes such an area is another question.) But as a general rule, the preferred alternative of most economists—and, in particular, the one most consistent with the Keynesian compact, because it leaves countries free to pursue both free-market and full-employment policies—is a floating exchange rate.

The virtues of such free floating, when it works, are not hard to demonstrate. The United States is well served by its general policy of benign neglect toward the foreign exchange value of the dollar; while the dollar-yen and dollar-euro rates may go through annoying gyrations, this annoyance is surely a small thing compared with the freedom of action the absence of an exchange rate commitment gives to the Federal Reserve—the ability to cut interest rates sharply and immediately when recession or financial crisis looms..

Better yet, consider the example of Australia. In 1996 an Australian dollar was worth almost $.80 in U.S. currency. By the late summer of 1998 it had fallen to little more than $.60. No surprise there: most of Australia's exports go either to Japan or to the troubled tigers. But Australia, except for a brief period in the summer (more on that next chapter), did not try to prop up its currency, either by buying it on the foreign exchange market or by raising interest rates. Instead, the currency's fall proved self-limiting: when the Aussie dollar fell, investors regarded it as an opportunity to invest cheaply in what they continued to regard as a solid economy. And this confidence appears justified by the "Australian miracle": despite its dependence on Asian markets, Australia has actually boomed for the past year.

But if Australia could so easily avoid getting caught up in its neighbors' economic catastrophe, why couldn't Indonesia or South Korea do the same?

The Double Standard

Imagine an economy that isn't perfect. (What economy is?) Maybe the government is running a budget deficit that, while not really threatening its solvency, is coming down more slowly than it should, or maybe banks with political connections have made too many loans to questionable borrowers. But, as far as anyone can tell by going over the numbers, there are no problems that cannot be dealt with given goodwill and a few years of stability.

Then, for some reason—perhaps an economic crisis on the other side of the world—investors become jittery and start pulling their money out en masse. Suddenly the country is in trouble, its stock market plunging, its interest rates soaring. You might think that savvy investors would see this as an opportunity to buy. After all, if the fundamentals haven't changed, doesn't this mean that assets are now undervalued? But, as we saw in Chapter 5, the answer is "not necessarily." The crash in asset values may cause previously sound banks to collapse; economic slump, high interest rates, and a devalued exchange rate may cause sound companies to go bankrupt; and, at worst, economic distress may cause political instability. Maybe buying when everyone else is rushing for the exits isn't such a good idea after all; maybe it's better to run for the exit yourself.

Thus it is possible in principle that a loss of confidence in a country can produce an economic crisis that justifies that loss of confidence—that countries may be vulnerable to what economists call "self-fulfilling speculative attacks." And while many economists used to be skeptical about the importance of such self-fulfilling crises, the experience of the 1990s in Latin America and Asia has settled those doubts, at least as a practical matter.

The funny thing is that once you take the possibility of self-fulfilling crises seriously, market psychology becomes crucial—so crucial that within limits the expectations, even the prejudices of investors become economic fundamentals—because believing makes it so.

Suppose, for example, that everyone is convinced that despite its remarkably high dependence on foreign capital (it has run large current account deficits of more than 4 percent of GDP for decades) Australia is basically a sound country, which can be counted on to be politically and economically stable. Then the market response to a decline in the Australian dollar is in effect to say, "Good, that's over, let's buy Australian," and the economy actually benefits. The market's good opinion is therefore confirmed.

On the other hand, suppose that despite twenty years of remarkable progress people are not quite convinced that Indonesia is no longer the country of *The Year of Living Dangerously*. Then when the rupiah falls they may say, "Oh, my God, they're reverting to the bad old days"; the resulting capital flight leads to financial, economic, and political crisis, and the market's bad opinion is similarly confirmed.

It seems, in other words, that there is a sort of double standard enforced by the markets. The common view among economists that floating rates are the best, if imperfect, solution to the international monetary trilemma was based on the experience of countries like Canada, Britain, and the United States. And sure enough, floating exchange rates do work pretty well for First World countries, because markets are prepared to give those countries the benefit of the doubt. But since 1994 one Third World country after another—Mexico, Thailand, Indonesia, Korea, and, most recently, Brazil—has discovered that it cannot expect the same treatment. Again and again, attempts to engage in moderate devaluations have led to a drastic collapse in confidence. And so now markets believe that devaluations in such countries are terrible things; and because markets believe this, they are.

It is this problem of confidence—a problem that Asians used to think did not apply to them, but which now clearly applies to all Third World countries—that ultimately explains why the Keynesian compact has been broken.

The Confidence Game

In the summer of 1998 Brazil was already suffering an economic slowdown; unemployment was rising, while inflation—Brazil's traditional ailment—had given way to price stability, and some were even talking of deflation. Then the collapse of economic reform in Russia triggered an attack on Brazil's *real* (why? See Chapter 7), and the country went to the United States and the IMF for help. What Brazil wanted was both money—it still had some $40 billion of foreign exchange reserves, but wanted a backup credit line—and, even more important, a sort of Good Housekeeping seal on its policies, something that would persuade nervous investors to stop running.

So what did the program—intended, remember, for a country with a slowing economy and no inflation to speak of—involve? Higher taxes, reduced government spending, and a continuation of extremely high interest rates (Brazil had raised rates to nearly 50 percent when the crisis began). In other words, the government undertook to pursue extremely tight monetary and fiscal policies, which absolutely guaranteed that the country would experience a nasty recession in 1999.

The program for Brazil was peculiarly extreme; it was almost like a caricature of the policies that had been introduced in Asia the preceding year. But like many caricatures, it emphasized the distinctive features of its subject. At the core of the policies imposed by Washington over the last few years, on one country after another, is an almost perfect inversion of the Keynesian compact: faced with an economic crisis, countries are urged to raise interest rates, slash spending, and increase taxes.

Why, sixty years after Keynes, would anybody think that it was a good idea to break so profoundly with the Keynesian compact? The answer lies in the double standard and the perceived need to win market confidence at all cost.

First of all, the Australian solution—just letting the currency slide—was ruled out. The fixed exchange rate between Brazil's *real* and the dollar had been a centerpiece of the country's reform program, the program that had brought price stability after generations of high inflation. To give up that fixed rate, both Brazil and Washington feared, would be devastating for investor confidence. True, one could make a good case that the *real* was, say, 20 percent overvalued and that a 20 percent devaluation would do the country far more good than harm. But nobody believed that a 20 percent devaluation was a possible strategy: as one U.S. official put it, "For developing countries, there are no small devaluations."

How was a devaluation of the *real* to be avoided? The IMF could supply money, which together with the country's own foreign exchange reserves could be used to support the currency in the markets. But this money would soon be gone unless something could be done to stop capital from fleeing. The only tool immediately at hand was to impose very high interest rates, high enough to persuade people to keep money in Brazil even though they suspected that its currency might end up devalued after all.

Nor was that all. When the markets decided that Brazil was a bad risk, they also decided that at the core of Brazil's problems was its large budget deficit. Now, you could question that assessment. Brazil's government actually didn't have all that much debt—considerably less, as a share of national income, than many European countries or than Japan. And much of the deficit was actually a consequence of the crisis: those high interest rates drove up the government's interest payments, while the slumping economy depressed tax revenue. (At "normal" levels of employment and interest rates, Brazil's budget deficit would have been quite modest.) But what was the use of arguing? Investors believed that Brazil would have a disastrous crisis unless the deficit was quickly reduced, and they were surely right, because they themselves would generate that crisis. (And indeed they did, in January 1999.)

The point is that, because speculative attacks can be self-justifying, following an economic policy that makes sense in terms of the fundamentals is not enough to assure market confidence. In fact, the need to win that confidence can actually prevent a country from following otherwise sensible policies and force it to follow policies that would normally seem perverse.

Now, consider the situation from the point of view of those clever economists who were making policy in Washington. They found themselves dealing with economies whose hold on investor confidence was fragile; almost by definition a country that has come to the United States and/or the IMF for help is one that has already experienced a devastating run on its currency and is at risk of another. The overriding objective of policy must therefore be to mollify market sentiment. But, because crises can be self-fulfilling, sound economic policy is not sufficient to gain market confidence; one must cater to the perceptions, the prejudices, the whims of the market. Or, rather, one must cater to what one *hopes* will be the perceptions of the market.

And that is how the Keynesian compact got broken: international economic policy ended up having very little to do with economics. It became an exercise in amateur psychology, in which the IMF and the Treasury Department tried to persuade countries to do things they hoped would be perceived by the market as favorable. No wonder the economics textbooks went right out the window as soon as the crisis hit.

Unfortunately, the textbook issues did not go away. Suppose that Washington was right, that a country threatened with an investor panic must raise interest rates, cut spending, and defend its currency to avoid devastating crisis. It still remains true that tight monetary and fiscal policies, together with an overvalued currency, produce recessions. What remedy does Washington offer? None. The perceived need to play the confidence game supersedes the normal concerns of economic policy. It sounds pretty crazy, and it is.

And so now we have solved the mystery with which Chapter 5 ended: why did policy fail to oppose the devastating feedback process that caused one economy after another to melt down? The answer is that those making policy believed that they had to play the confidence game, and that this meant following macroeconomic policies that exacerbated slumps instead of relieving them.

But was it really necessary to play this game?

Did the IMF Make the Situation Worse?

Nobody likes the International Monetary Fund; if anyone did, it would be a bad sign. For the IMF is a "lender of last resort" for national governments: it is the place they go for money when they are in trouble. And lenders of last resort are supposed to practice tough love: to give you what you need rather than what you want, and to force you to pull yourself together in the process. A warm, cuddly IMF wouldn't be doing its job.

But the converse isn't necessarily true: just because people hate the IMF doesn't mean that it is doing its job well. And since the onset of the Asian crisis there have been many complaints about the IMF's role. Quite a few people think that the IMF (and the U.S. Treasury Department, which de facto largely dictates the IMF's policies) actually caused the crisis, or that it mishandled the crisis in a way that made it far worse than it needed to be. Are they right?

Let's start with the easy part: two things that the IMF clearly did do wrong.

First, when the IMF was called in to Thailand, Indonesia, and Korea, it quickly demanded that they practice fiscal austerity—that they raise taxes and cut spending, in order to avoid large budget deficits. It was hard to understand why this was part of the program, since in Asia (unlike in Brazil a year later) nobody but the IMF seemed to regard budget deficits as an important problem. And the attempt to meet these budget guidelines had a doubly negative effect on the countries: where the guidelines were met, the effect was to worsen the recession by reducing demand; where they were not met, the effect was to add, gratuitously, to the sense that things were out of control, and hence to feed the market panic.

Second, the IMF demanded "structural" reform—that is, changes that went well beyond monetary and fiscal policy—as a condition for loans to afflicted economies. Some of these reforms, like closing bad banks, were arguably relevant to the financial crisis. Others, like demanding that Indonesia eliminate the practice of giving presidential cronies lucrative monopolies in some businesses, seem to have had little if anything to do with the IMF's mandate. True, the monopoly on cloves (which Indonesians like to put in their cigarettes) was a bad thing, a glaring example of crony capitalism at work. But what did it have to do with the run on the rupiah?

If you had asked IMF officials at the time what they thought they were doing, they would have answered that it was all part of the business of rebuilding confidence. Budget deficits were not a market concern at the moment, but they thought they soon would be; and they also thought that it was important for countries to make a highly visible show of combating cronyism and corruption, to convince markets that they really had changed their ways. One might almost describe this as the view that governments had to show their seriousness by inflicting pain on themselves—whether or not that pain had any direct relevance to the immediate problems—because only thus could they regain the market's trust.

If that was the theory, it turns out to have been quite wrong. The budget guidelines were eventually relaxed, and nobody minded; at the time of writing, markets seem to be bullish once again on Korea, even though structural reform appears to have stalled. Meanwhile, the sheer breadth of IMF demands, aside from raising suspicions that the United States was trying to use the crisis to impose its ideological vision on Asia, more or less guaranteed a prolonged period of wrangling between Asian governments and their rescuers, a period during which the crisis of confidence steadily worsened.

So the IMF bungled two important pieces of the rescue. But the really big issues involved interest rates and exchange rates. Did it bungle these, too?

Here's what the IMF did: in Asia (as opposed to Brazil, which as I said was a sort of caricature of the Asian programs) it did not tell countries to defend the values of their currencies at all cost. But it did tell them to raise interest rates, initially to very high levels, in an attempt to persuade investors to keep their money in place. Some vociferous critics of the IMF—most notably Harvard's Jeffrey Sachs—say that this was very much the wrong thing to do. Sachs believes, in effect, that Asian countries could and should have behaved like Australia, simply letting their currencies decline until they started to look cheap to investors, and that if they had the great slump would never have happened.

What the IMF says in response is that Asia is not Australia: that to let the currencies fall unchecked would have led to "hyperdevaluations," and that the result would have been both massive financial distress (because so many businesses had debt denominated in dollars) and soaring inflation. The trouble with this rationale is, of course, that the massive financial distress happened anyway, thanks to high interest rates and the recession they helped cause; so the IMF at best avoided one vicious circle only by starting another.

This same observation undermines the argument by many right-wing critics of the IMF, that it *should* have told countries to defend their original exchange rates at all cost. This could indeed have avoided the collapse of confidence in Asian *currencies*; but it would have done nothing to prevent the collapse of confidence in Asian *economies*, and the economic meltdown would probably still have happened.

Would simply letting the currencies fall have worked better? Sachs argues that by *not* raising interest rates, governments would have avoided feeding the financial panic; the result would have been modest, tolerable devaluations and a far better economic outcome. This argument, which seemed implausible to many people (myself included) at the time of the Asian crisis, gained a bit more credibility in January 1999, when Washington quite clearly bungled Brazil; but more about that in Chapter 8.

Surely, however, the bottom line is that there were no good choices. The rules of the New World Order, it seemed, offered developing countries no way out. And so it was really nobody's fault that things turned out so badly.

Which is not to say that there were no villains in the plot.

■

Masters of the Universe:

Hedge Funds and

Other Villains

I n the bad old days, before the New World Order, the figure of the evil speculator—the malefactor of great wealth who manipulates markets to the detriment of honest workers—was a staple of popular culture. But with the fall of Communism, the successes of globalization, and the general revival of faith in free markets, the evil speculator went the way of witches and warlocks: serious people stopped believing in his existence. Oh, nobody but the most extreme defenders of laissez-faire denied that there were cases in which people traded on inside information and maybe even manipulated the price of a stock here, a commodity there. But surely this was petty crime; the big financial events, those that shaped the destiny of nations, involved markets far too large for conspiracy theories to be plausible. No individuals or small groups could really affect the currency value of even a middle-sized economy, could they?

Well, maybe they could. One of the most bizarre aspects of the economic crisis of the last few years has been the prominent part played by "hedge funds," investment institutions that are able to take temporary control of assets far in excess of their owners' wealth. Without question hedge funds, in both their success and their failure, have rocked world markets; and in at least a few cases, the evil speculator has staged a comeback.

The Nature of the Beast

Hedge funds don't hedge. Indeed, they do more or less the opposite. To hedge, says *Webster's*, is "to try to avoid or lessen loss by making counterbalancing bets, investments, etc." That is, one hedges in order to make sure that market fluctuations do *not* affect one's wealth.

What hedge funds do, by contrast, is precisely to try to make the most of market fluctuations. The way they do this is typically to go short in some assets—that is, promise to deliver them at a fixed price at some future date—and go long in others. Profits come if the shorted assets fall in price (so that they can be delivered cheaply) or the purchased assets rise, or both.*

The good news about this kind of financial play is that it can deliver a very high return to the hedge fund's investors. The reason is that the fund can take a position much larger than the amount of money its owners put in, since it buys its "long" position mainly with the cash raised from creating its "short" posi-

---

*The terminology of "short" versus "long" positions is jargon, but too useful a shorthand to be avoided in this book. Basically, to go long in something is to put yourself in a position to gain if its price rises—which is what the ordinary investor does when buying stock, real estate, or anything else. To go short in something is to put yourself in a position to gain if its price *falls*. To sell a stock short, one borrows the stock from its owner with a promise to return it later— then one sells it. This means that the stock must be repurchased before the due date; the short-seller is betting that its price will have fallen by then. Meanwhile, the short-seller has acquired extra cash, which can be invested in something else—that is, he takes a long position in some other asset.

Of course, the owners of the borrowed assets have to be reassured that the short-seller will actually have enough cash to buy the asset back, so they will want some kind of reassurance that he has enough wealth to deliver on his promise. When investors who engage in a lot of short-selling suffer heavy losses, they typically find that they are no longer able to borrow as much as they could before. When such investors play a large role in the market, this can have interesting consequences, as we will see shortly.

tion. Indeed, the only reason it needs to have any capital at all is to persuade the counterparts of its asset shorts that it will actually be able to deliver on its promises. Hedge funds with good reputations have been able to take positions as much as a hundred times as large as their owners' capital; that means that a 1 percent rise in the price of their assets, or decline in the price of their liabilities, doubles that capital.

The bad news, of course, is that a hedge fund can also lose money very efficiently. Market movements that might not seem all that large to ordinary investors can quickly wipe out a hedge fund's capital, or at least cause it to lose its shorts—that is, induce those who have lent it stocks or other assets to demand that they be returned.

How big are hedge funds? Nobody really knows, because until quite recently nobody thought it was necessary to find out. Indeed, until last fall hedge funds—unlike almost every other financial institution—were pretty much left alone by regulators. One reason was that the investors themselves did not seem to need protection: most hedge funds had a large minimum investment (some as high as $10 million), so that their investors were normally wealthy individuals, who the government figured could take care of themselves. And hedge funds, unlike banks, did not seem to be key links in the financial system, whose soundness had to be monitored in the public interest. Last but not least, hedge funds—needing only a limited amount of capital, from a small number of people—could and did operate "offshore," establishing legal residence in accommodating jurisdictions to free themselves from annoying interference. To police their operations would not have been impossible, but it would have been difficult; and until last year the general consensus, at least in the United States, was that there was no need.

But in a way that was a strange attitude, because even before the recent series of crises one famous hedge fund had given an impressive demonstration of just how much influence a highly leveraged investor can have.

The Legend of George Soros

George Soros, a Hungarian refugee turned American entrepreneur, founded his Quantum Fund in 1969. By 1992 he was a billionaire, already famous as the "world's greatest investor," and already celebrated for the generosity and creativity of his philanthropic activities. But Soros—who is a man with intellectual as well as financial ambitions, who would like the world to take his philosophical pronouncements as seriously as it takes his business acumen—wanted more. As he himself says, he went in search of a business coup that would not only make money but generate publicity for himself, publicity that he could use to promote his nonbusiness ventures.

He found his opportunity in the state of Britain that summer. In 1990 Britain had joined the European Monetary System's Exchange Rate Mechanism (ERM), a system of fixed exchange rates that was intended as a way station en route to a unified European currency. Like the unhappy continents in our globo parable, however, Britain found that it did not like the monetary policy it was forced to follow. At the time Europe did not have a European Central Bank; while there was a legal fiction of symmetry among nations, in practice everyone matched the monetary policy of Germany's Bundesbank. And Germany was, literally, in a different place from the rest of Europe: having just reunified, it was compelled to spend large sums on the attempted reconstruction of East Germany. Fearing that this expenditure would be inflationary, the Bundesbank maintained high interest rates to prevent its own economy from overheating. Meanwhile Britain, which probably entered the ERM at too high a rate in any case, was in a deep recession, and its government was facing growing popular dissatisfaction. Officials strenuously denied that they would consider dropping out of the ERM; but there was a nagging doubt about whether they really meant it.

It was a situation ready-made for a currency crisis; and Soros decided not only to bet on such a crisis but to provoke one.

The mechanics of the bet were conceptually simple, if extremely complex in detail. The first stage had to be low-profile, even secretive, as Quantum Fund quietly established credit lines that would allow it to borrow about $15 billion worth of British pounds and to convert that sum into dollars at will. Then, once the fund was already substantially long dollars and short pounds, the attack had to turn noisy: Soros would be as ostentatious as possible about short-selling the pound, give interviews to financial newspapers declaring his belief that the pound would soon be devalued, and so on. If all went well, this would generate a run on the pound by other investors, a run that would force the British government to give in and devalue.

It worked. Soros's high-profile assault on the pound began in August. Within weeks Britain had spent nearly $50 billion in the foreign exchange markets to defend the pound, to no avail. In mid-September the government raised interest rates to defend the currency, but this proved politically unacceptable; after only three days Britain dropped out of the ERM, and the pound was set floating (where it remains to this day). And Soros not only made roughly a billion dollars in quick capital gains, but established himself as perhaps the most famous speculator of all time.

But what did Soros actually do? There are three questions here.

First, did Soros undermine a currency that would otherwise have maintained its value? Probably not. The fact is that pressures on the pound were building steadily, and many economists (though not many market participants) already suspected that Britain was not long for the ERM. Nobody can prove this assertion, but my strong belief is that Britain's attempt to join the continental monetary club was doomed, Soros or no Soros.

But in that case, did Soros at least move up the timetable, causing the pound to devalue sooner than it otherwise would have? Almost surely yes, but the question is by how much. Again, one cannot prove this one way or the other, but my own guess is that economic conditions were moving Britain in the direction of a near-term exit from the ERM in any case and that Soros moved up the timetable by only a few weeks.

Finally, did Soros do his victims any harm? The government of Prime Minster John Major never recovered from the humiliation. But, it is actually possible to argue that Soros did the British nation as a whole a favor. The decline of the pound did not create an economic crisis: the currency stabilized spontaneously at about 15 percent below its previous value. Freed of the need to support the pound, the British government was able to reduce interest rates. (Chancellor of the Exchequer Norman Lamont declared that he had been "singing in the bath" with relief over the end of a currency peg he had declared absolutely inviolable only a few days before. His relief was premature; most Britons gained from the devaluation, but he himself was soon forced to resign.) The combination of lower interest rates and a more competitive exchange rate soon led to a strong recovery in the British economy, which within a few years had brought unemployment down to levels its neighbors regarded as unreachable. For the ordinary Briton, Soros's attack on the pound brought mainly good news.

So it wasn't such a terrible story, after all. True, Europeans who were deeply committed to the cause of monetary union regarded the events of 1992 as a tragedy; the French, who basically fought off the speculative attacks of 1992 and 1993 (they briefly allowed the franc to float, but soon brought it back into the ERM band) were heard to mutter old-fashioned denunciations of currency speculators as agents of evil. But in the dominant Anglo-Saxon world of policy discussion, the story of Soros and the pound was not regarded as any sort of worrisome omen.

All that changed when the Asian crisis hit, and it turned out that the results of speculation could be considerably less benign.

The Madness of Prime Minister Mahathir

Try to imagine how it must have felt. He had managed his country's awkward ethnic politics with consummate skill: he pacified the country's Malay majority with the *bumiputra* ("son of the soil") program offering that majority preferential economic treatment, yet did so without driving out the commercially crucial Chinese minority. He had made the nation a favorite site for multinational branch plants even while pursuing an independent, somewhat anti-Western foreign policy that played well with a mostly Islamic populace. And under his leadership the country had shared fully in the Asian miracle: as its economy surged, foreign businessmen, from Bill Gates on down, came courting, and in the summer of 1997 *Time* declared him one of the world's top one hundred "technology leaders."

Oh, there were a few criticisms. Some of his friends and family members seemed to have gotten rich rather easily; some foreigners accused him of grandiosity, with his insistence on building the world's tallest building, on constructing a new capital and a massive new "technology corridor." But on the whole he had every reason to feel well satisfied with his achievements.

And then, with shocking suddenness, things went sour. His undisciplined neighbors had a currency crisis—well, that was their problem. But then money started flooding out of his country, too; and he was faced with the humiliating choice between letting the currency plunge or raising interest rates, either of which would put many of those hard-built businesses in severe financial straits. How could this happen?

So in a way we should not blame Mahathir Mohamad, prime minister of Malaysia, for his susceptibility to conspiracy theories. After all, it was common knowledge that George Soros had engineered the run on the pound five years earlier; and Quantum Fund had certainly been speculating in Southeast Asian currencies over the past several years. What was more natural than to blame the famous speculator for his woes? One might even call it a bit of poetic justice: since Soros, by his own account, had attacked the pound as much for the notoriety as the money; now he was being hoisted by his own petard.

Nonetheless, Mahathir clearly should have kept his mouth shut. At a time when confidence in his economy was already plunging, the sight of the prime minister raving about an American conspiracy against Asia—and broadly hinting that it was in fact, yes, a *Jewish* conspiracy—was not what the money doctors would have prescribed.

And it also happened not to be true. Quantum Fund had speculated against Thailand, but then so had lots of people. The speculative flight of capital from Malaysia, it turns out, was carried out largely by Malaysians themselves—in particular, some of the very same businessmen who had gotten rich thanks to Mahathir's favor.

Nonetheless, Mahathir continued to press his case, attacking Soros in press conferences and speeches. Only after several months had gone by, and the state of the Malaysian economy began to look truly alarming, did he become relatively quiet, afraid to disturb the markets. Perhaps he also became aware that most of the world thought his complaints were silly; conspiracies like that just don't happen in the real world.

And then one did.

The Attack on Hong Kong

Hong Kong has long had a special place in the hearts of free-market enthusiasts. At a time when most Third World countries believed that protectionism and government planning were the way to develop, Hong Kong had free trade and a policy of letting entrepreneurs rip—and showed that such a wide-open economy could grow at rates development theorists had never imagined possible. The city-state also led the revival of currency boards, which some conservatives like to imagine are the first step on the road back to the gold standard. Year after year the conservative Heritage Foundation has given Hong Kong top ranking on its "index of economic freedom."

But Hong Kong has suffered from the Asian crisis. It is hard to find any fault in the city's own management: more than any other in the region, its economy was run according to the rule of law, with well-regulated banks and conservative budget policies. There was little sign of rampant cronyism before the crisis, nor was there, in the first year, any panicky flight of capital. Still, the city was clearly in the wrong place at the wrong time.

As its neighbors slumped, business suffered: Japanese stopped popping over for shopping trips, Southeast Asian firms stopped buying the services of Hong Kong banks. Worse yet, Hong Kong's strict currency board system meant that the exchange rate was fixed solidly at 7.8 to the U.S. dollar, even as much of the rest of Asia devalued; suddenly Hong Kong was far more expensive than Bangkok or even Tokyo. The result was a deepening recession, the worst in memory.

Inevitably, nagging doubts began to surface. Would Hong Kong really defend its exchange rate at all costs? Some Hong Kong businessmen openly urged the Monetary Authority to devalue the currency, to make their costs competitive again. Such demands were dismissed, and the government declared the rate inviolate; but then so had the government of Britain in 1992. Also, what about China? Asia's giant largely escaped the first wave of the crisis, thanks mainly to its currency controls (see Chapter 8), but by the summer of 1998 signs of an economic slowdown were emerging, and with them rumors that China's currency, too, might be devalued—which would put Hong Kong under far greater strain.

Some might see all of this as bad news; but some hedge funds saw it as an opportunity.

There are, for obvious reasons, no hard numbers on just what happened in August and September of 1998, but here is the way the story is told, both by Hong Kong officials and by market players. A small group of hedge funds—rumored to include Soros's Quantum Fund and Julian Robertson's less famous but equally influential Tiger Fund, although officials named no names—began a "double play" against Hong Kong. They sold Hong Kong stocks short—that is, they borrowed stocks from their owners, then sold them for Hong Kong dollars (with a promise to those owners to buy the stocks back and return them, of course—as well as a "rental fee" for the use of the stocks in the meantime). Then they traded those Hong Kong dollars for U.S. dollars. In effect, they were betting that one of two things would happen. Either the Hong Kong dollar would be devalued, so that they would make money on their currency speculation; or the Hong Kong Monetary Authority would defend its currency by raising interest rates, which would drive down the local stock market, and they would make money off their stock market short position.

But in the view of Hong Kong officials, the hedge funds weren't just betting on these events: like Soros in 1992, they were doing their best to make them happen. The sales of Hong Kong dollars were ostentatious, carried out in large blocks, regularly timed, so as to make sure that everyone in the market noticed. Again without naming names, Hong Kong officials also claim that the hedge funds paid reporters and editors to run stories suggesting that the HK dollar or the Chinese renminbi, or both, were on the verge of devaluation. In other words, they were deliberately trying to start a run on the currency.

Did the hedge funds actually conspire together? It's possible: while an explicit agreement to manipulate the price of, say, Microsoft stock would land you in jail, a comparable conspiracy against the Hong Kong stock market (which has about the same capitalization) apparently falls through the legal cracks. It's also possible there was no contact at all. But more likely there were hints and winks, a few generalities over a round of golf or an expensive bottle of wine. After all, there weren't that many players, and they all knew how the game worked.

Indeed, some observers see the shadow of a still wider plot. The Hong Kong Four (or Five, or whatever) had other plays going at the same time. They were short yen—because interest rates in Japan were low, and they thought the yen might well plunge along with the Hong Kong dollar—as well as Australian dollars, Canadian dollars, and so on. And they became big, ostentatious sellers of some of these other currencies too. So you could think of Hong Kong as only the centerpiece of a play against much of the Asia-Pacific region, indeed quite possibly the largest market conspiracy of all time.

And it all looked quite likely to succeed. After all, what could Hong Kong do? Its stock market was large compared with that of most developing countries, but not compared with the resources of the hedge funds; reports are that the combined short position of the alleged conspirators was about $30 billion, which would be the equivalent of short-selling roughly $1.5 *trillion* in the U.S. stock market. Moreover, the Hong Kong market was wide open, and likely to remain so: a city whose livelihood depended precisely on its reputation as a place where people could do as they liked with their money, free from arbitrary government interference, would not even dare to flirt with controls on capital flight. All in all, it looked like a brilliant plan, with very high chances of success.

Unexpectedly, Hong Kong fought back.

The main weapon in that fight was a novel, unconventional use of the Hong Kong Monetary Authority's funds. The HKMA, as it happened, had huge resources. Remember, Hong Kong has a currency board, so that every 7.8 Hong Kong dollars of money in circulation is backed by one U.S. dollar in reserves; but it turns out that the HKMA has actually banked far more dollars than it needs for that purpose. How could this wealth be deployed against the hedge funds? By using it to buy local stocks—thereby driving their prices up and causing the hedge funds, which had sold those stocks short, to lose money. Of course, in order to be effective these purchases would have to be on a large scale, comparable to or even greater than the hedge funds' short sales. But the authorities certainly had the resources to make such purchases.

Why, then, hadn't the hedge funds expected this response? Because they didn't think the Hong Kong government would be willing to risk the inevitable reaction from conservatives horrified that such a free-market paragon would try to manipulate market prices. And the reaction was fierce indeed. The government's actions were "insane," thundered Milton Friedman; the Heritage Foundation formally removed the city-state's designation as a bastion of economic freedom; newspaper stories linked Hong Kong with Malaysia, which had just imposed draconian capital controls. Finance Secretary Donald Tsang began touring the world, trying to explain the actions to investors and reassure them that his government was as pro-capitalism as ever; but it was an uphill fight.

For a time the hedge funds seem to have expected that the reaction would force the Hong Kong authorities to back down. They rolled over their short positions (that is, paid the original owners of the stock additional fees for the right to put off their return) and settled in to wait the government out. The government then upped the ante, instituting new rules that restricted short-selling, thereby forcing the Hong Kong investors who had rented out their stocks to call them in; this forced the hedge funds to unwind their positions, but raised further howls of outrage.

And then the whole Hong Kong issue faded away, because a bizarre series of events around the world forced the hedge funds themselves to curtail their activities.

The Potemkin Economy

In 1787, the empress Catherine of Russia toured her empire's southern provinces. According to legend, her chief minister Grigori Aleksandrovich Potemkin stayed one day ahead, setting up false fronts that made wretched villages look prosperous, then dismantling the props and leapfrogging them to the next destination. Ever since, the term "Potemkin village" has been used to refer to apparently happy scenes that are in reality nothing but facade, bearing no relation to what really lies behind them.

It is entirely appropriate, then, that in the second half of the 1990s Russia itself became a sort of Potemkin economy.

Nobody has found the transition from socialism to capitalism easy, but Russia has found it harder than most. For the most part its economy seems caught in a sort of limbo, having lost whatever guidance central planning used to provide, yet without having managed to achieve a working market system either. Even the things that used to work to some extent no longer function: factories that used to produce low-quality goods now produce nothing at all, collective farms have become even less productive than they were before, and the dreary Brezhnev years now seem like a golden age. There are hundreds of thousands of highly skilled programmers, engineers, scientists, mathematicians, but they cannot find decent work. Still, the country is not without resources: natural gas, oil, and gold all provide a steady stream of hard-currency earnings, and foreign investors still dream of the fortunes that could be made there if the nation's potential were somehow unleashed.

Those dreams, however, are receding. Boris Yeltsin made Russia into a democracy, at least for the time being; but he also turned it into a kleptocracy, a government of thieves. A small group of "oligarchs," who use political influence to acquire economic privilege and wealth to buy politicians, have ended up dominating the money-making parts of the economy, having pretty much hijacked the country's "privatization" program to their own enrichment. One might at least have hoped that, having stolen the country, the oligarchs would then try to run it as a paying business; but instead they have acted as short-term looters, extracting whatever they could and shipping the money out of the country. (Remember how inflows of capital necessarily imply a trade deficit? In recent years Russia has consistently run large trade *surpluses*, as export earnings are used, not to pay for imports, but to build up overseas bank accounts.) In particular, the oligarchs—the only Russians who really could pay considerably more in taxes—have chosen not to (remember, they own many of the politicians), leaving the government in a permanent fiscal crisis, forced to borrow money at increasingly usurious rates.

It is a sorry state of affairs, but Russia has one last asset: as the heir of the Soviet Union, it still has a massive arsenal of nuclear weapons. It has not explicitly threatened to sell nukes to the highest bidder, but the risk that it might has conditioned Western policy, making the U.S. government anxious to put the best face on things. Long after most informed people had become thoroughly cynical, the United States continued to hope that

Russia's reformers would somehow manage to complete the stalled transition, that the oligarchs would stop being so selfish or at least so shortsighted; and the U.S. government has bullied the IMF into lending money to Russia to buy time for stabilization plans that somehow never materialize. (*The Medley Report*, an international economic newsletter, commented that the United States was not, as some said, throwing money down a rathole; it was throwing money down a missile silo.)

The apparent ability of Russia to use its nuclear arms as collateral, in turn, encouraged high-rolling foreign investors to take a risk and put money into Russia. Everyone knew that the ruble might well be devalued, perhaps massively, or that the Russian government might simply default on its debts. But it seemed a good bet that before that happened the West would step in with yet another emergency cash injection. Since Russian government debt was offering extremely high interest rates, eventually reaching 150 percent, the bet was an appealing one to investors with a high tolerance for risk—notably hedge funds.

However, it turned out that the bet wasn't that good, after all. In the summer of 1998 Russia's financial situation unraveled faster than expected. In August, George Soros (!) suggested publicly that Russia devalue the ruble and then establish a currency board; his remarks triggered a run on the currency, an inadequate Mexican-style devaluation, and then a combination of currency collapse and debt moratorium. And the West had apparently had enough: there was no rescue this time. Suddenly claims on Russia could be sold, if at all, for only a fraction of their face value, and billions of dollars had been lost. (What happened to that nuclear collateral? Good question; let's not think about it.)

In sheer dollar terms the money lost in Russia was quite trivial—no more than is lost when, for example, the U.S. stock market falls by a fraction of a percent, which it does almost every other day. But these losses fell heavily on a small group of highly leveraged financial operators, which meant that they had almost ridiculously large effects on the rest of the world.

Indeed, for a few weeks it looked as if Russia's financial collapse would drag down the whole world.

The Panic of 1998

In the summer of 1998 the balance sheets of the world's hedge funds were not only huge but immensely complex. Still, there was a pattern. Typically these funds were short in assets that were safe—not likely to plunge in value—and liquid—that is, easy to sell if you needed cash. At the same time, they were long in assets that were risky and illiquid. Thus a hedge fund might be short German government debt, which is safe and easy to sell, and long Danish mortgage-backed securities (indirect claims on houses), which are a bit more risky and a lot harder to sell at short notice. Or they might be short Japanese bonds and long Russian debt.

The general principle here was that historically markets have tended to place a rather high premium on both safety and liquidity, because small investors were risk-averse and never knew when they might need to cash out. This offered an opportunity to big operators, who could minimize the risk by careful diversification (buying a mix of assets, so that gains on one would normally offset losses on another), and who would not normally find themselves suddenly in need of cash. It was largely by exploiting these margins that hedge funds made so much money, year after year.

By 1998, however, many people understood this basic idea, and competition among the hedge funds themselves had made it increasingly difficult to make money. Some hedge funds actually started returning investors' money, declaring that they could not find enough profitable opportunities to use it. But they also tried to find new opportunities by stretching even further, taking complex positions that appeared on the surface to be hugely risky, but that supposedly were cunningly constructed to minimize the chance of losses.

What nobody realized until it happened was that the competition among hedge funds to exploit ever narrower profit opportunities had created a sort of financial doomsday machine.

Here's how it worked. Suppose that some hedge fund—call it Relativity Fund—has taken a big bet in Russian government debt. Then Russia defaults, and it loses a billion dollars or so. This makes the investors who are the counterparts of its short positions—the people who have lent it stocks and bonds, to be returned in future—nervous, so they demand their assets back. However, Relativity doesn't actually have those assets on hand; it must buy them back, which means that it must sell other assets to get the necessary cash. And since it is such a big player in the markets, when it starts selling the prices of the things it has invested in go down.

Meanwhile, Relativity's rival, the Pussycat Fund, has also invested in many of the same things. So when Relativity is forced into sudden large sales, this means big losses for Pussycat as well; it too finds itself forced to "cover its shorts" by selling, driving the prices of other assets down. In so doing, it creates a problem for the Elizabethan Fund . . . and so on down the line.

If all this reminds you of the story of Asia's financial meltdown, as I told it in Chapter 5, it should: at a fundamental level it was the same kind of process, involving a vicious circle of plunging prices and imploding balance sheets. Nobody thought that such a thing could happen in the modern world, but it did, and the consequences were startling.

You see, it turned out that the hedge funds had been so assiduous about arbitraging away liquidity and risk premia that for many illiquid assets they *were* the market; when they all tried to sell at once, there were no alternative buyers. And so after years of steadily narrowing, liquidity and risk premia suddenly surged to unheard-of levels. By late September, twenty-nine-year U.S. government bonds—a perfectly safe asset, in the sense that if the U.S. government goes, so does everything else—were offering significantly higher interest rates than thirty-year bonds, which are traded in a larger market and are therefore slightly easier to sell. Corporate bonds normally must offer higher

returns than U.S. government debt, but the spread had suddenly widened by several percentage points. And commercial
mortgage-backed securities—the financial instruments that
indirectly fund most nonresidential real estate construction—
could not be sold at all. At one meeting I attended, participants
asked a Federal Reserve official who described the situation
what could be done to resolve it. "Pray," he replied.

In fact, luckily, the Fed did more than that. First of all, it
engineered the rescue of the most famous casualty among the
hedge funds: Connecticut-based Long Term Capital Management.

The saga of LTCM is even more remarkable than the legend
of George Soros. Soros is a figure in a long tradition, that of the
swashbuckling financial raider—not that different, when you
get to essentials, from Jim Fisk or Jay Gould. The managers at
Long Term Capital, however, were quintessentially modern
types: nerd savants, using formulas and computers to outsmart
the market. The firm boasted two Nobel laureates on its pay-
roll, and many of their best students. They believed that by
carefully studying the historical correlations between assets,
they could construct clever portfolios—long some assets, short
others—that yielded high returns with much less risk than people imagined. And year after year they delivered, with such reg-
ularity that, it turned out, people who lent them money stopped
even asking whether the firm really had enough capital to be a
safe partner.

Then the markets went crazy.

It is still unclear whether the losses that LTCM suffered were
the result of once-in-a-lifetime shocks that could not have been
anticipated, or whether the computer models they used were
naive in not allowing for the occasional large market distur-
bance. (And also whether this naïveté, if that was what it was,
was deliberate—moral hazard again.) Whatever the cause, by
September the company was facing margin calls—demands
that it either put more cash on deposit with the lenders or pay
up in full—that it could not meet. And suddenly it became
clear that LTCM had become so large a player in the markets

that if it failed, and its positions were liquidated, it might pre-cipitate a full-scale panic.

Something had to be done. In the end, no public money was required: the New York Fed was able to persuade a group of investors to take over majority ownership of LTCM in return for a desperately needed injection of cash; and as it turned out, once markets had calmed down again the banks actually ended up doing quite well in the deal.

Even with the rescue, however, it was by no means a fore-gone conclusion that the crisis would be surmounted. When the Fed cut interest rates by only 0.25 percent at its regularly scheduled September meeting, the size of the cut disappointed the markets, and the already troubled financial situation started to look like a runaway panic. Suddenly people were starting to draw analogies between the financial crisis and the bank runs that plunged the United States into the Great Depression; J. P. Morgan even went so far as to flatly predict a severe recession in 1999.

But the Fed had a trick up its sleeve. Normally interest rate changes take place only when the Federal Open Market Com-mittee meets, roughly every six weeks. In that September meet-ing, however, the committee had granted Alan Greenspan the discretionary power to cut interest rates a further quarter point whenever necessary. On October 15 he surprised the markets by announcing that cut—and, miraculously, the markets ral-lied. When the Fed cut rates yet again at its next meeting, the panic turned into euphoria. By the end of 1998 all the unusual liquidity premia had vanished, and the stock market was once again setting new records.

It is important to realize that even now Fed officials are not quite sure how they pulled this rescue off. At the height of the crisis it seemed entirely possible that cutting interest rates would be entirely ineffectual—after all, if nobody can borrow, what difference does it make what the price would be if they could? And if everyone had believed that the world was coming to an end, their panic might—as in so many other countries— have ended up being a self-fulfilling prophecy. In retrospect

Greenspan seemed to have been like a general who rides out in front of his demoralized army, waves his sword and shouts encouragement, and somehow turns the tide of battle: well done, but not something you would want to count on working next time.

Indeed, some Fed officials fret that the public may be over-rating their abilities—a new form of moral hazard, says one Greenspan adviser, based on the belief that the Fed chairman could bail the economy and the markets out of any crisis.

Perhaps that overestimation of the Fed played a role in the global recovery of confidence that took place in the late fall of last year; but there was also, finally, some good news from Asia.

E I G H T

•

Bottoming Out?

F OR the first year after the baht was devalued, the news from Asia was almost unrelievedly bad; each month brought economic tidings that were not only worse than anyone expected but worse than anyone could have imagined. Starting in the summer of 1998, however, this black picture faded to gray, with even a few patches of blue. Partly this simply reflected how accustomed we had all become to disaster stories; people were agreeably surprised to hear that the pace of economic decline had slowed, that things were getting worse more slowly. But there was even some actual positive news: interest rates in Asia were down, stock markets were up, and—in Korea, at least—some genuine recovery in the real economy seemed to be materializing.

At the same time, however, the era of crisis was far from over. As this book was going to press, Brazil's economic program—which I had expected to unravel sometime in 1999, but not so soon—came apart at the seams, and the *real* lost more than 40 percent of its dollar value in barely more than two weeks. Some Asian economies—Hong Kong's in particular—were still spiraling downward.

Why did Asia apparently "bottom out" in late 1998? Did this mark the beginning of the end of the crisis, or merely the end of the beginning?

Dead Tiger Bounce?

Imagine a long, closely spaced line of cars speeding along a highway at, say, 60 miles an hour. Then, suddenly, the lead car reaches a stretch of bad road, which forces it to slow to half its former speed. What happens?

Unless the drivers have inhumanly fast reactions, the line of cars will not slow smoothly to 30 mph. The second driver will take some time to realize that the car in front of him has braked, by which time the gap between the cars will have narrowed considerably; he will therefore temporarily have to slow to something less than 30, perhaps 20, to reestablish his position. The car behind him will have to slow down even more, and so on. As the "shock wave" from the worsened road ahead propagates back down the line, many drivers will actually be forced to come to a complete stop for a time—if they do not rear-end the vehicle ahead of them. The average speed of the cars will drop, not from 60 to 30, but from 60 to something like 15 or even 10. But eventually this shock effect will dissipate; even if the road is still bad, the average speed will gradually rise to 30 again.

Something similar happens to economies. When the fundamentals worsen, there is often a drastic initial effect, followed by a partial recovery. Economists sometimes call it the "accelerator principle" (yes, it works for deceleration too); it plays a role in most business slumps, and explains why even the worst slumps are normally followed by a spontaneous partial bounce back. After four years of catastrophic decline, the U.S. economy grew by more than 8 percent in 1934; after the terrible first year of debt crisis, Mexico grew more than 3 percent in 1984. In both cases, of course, there was still a long stretch of rough road ahead: America did not fully emerge from the Great Depression until 1941; Mexico, from its debt crisis until 1990.

In garden-variety recessions the accelerator principle oper-
ates mainly because of inventory effects. When consumer
demand drops (or merely grows more slowly than expected),
businesses are caught by surprise; unsold items pile up on the
shelves and in the warehouses. To get rid of the excess inventory, companies must temporarily cut their production sharply,
laying off workers and buying less from suppliers; this in turn
further reduces consumer demand, and so on. For a time, the
recession therefore feeds on itself. But eventually inventories
are reduced to normal levels, and production recovers part of
the lost ground, even if the original causes of the slowdown
have not been cured. This conventional inventory accelerator
was part of the story for Asia; but less conventional effects were
also at work.

One example was the temporary credit crunch that afflicted
many businesses. In the first few months of the crisis, banks
were in trouble everywhere in Asia—partly because they had
come to count on an inflow of foreign funds that suddenly went
into reverse, partly because local depositors were nervous and
pulled their money out of the banks. Without money to lend,
banks could no longer extend or even maintain credit lines to
their business customers; and many businesses, even those still
making a profit, found themselves strapped for cash, unable to
pay for raw materials. The situation was particularly acute for
exporting firms, which should have been in a position to do
very well thanks to devalued currencies, but which initially
found themselves unable to take advantage of these opportunities. The disappointing export response, in turn, helped make
foreign investors wary and force governments to keep interest
rates high.

Over time, however, companies found ways around this
problem—they borrowed money from families and friends, or
simply accumulated enough cash to operate on a pay-as-you-go
basis, and the credit crunch faded away.

Another example of spontaneous recovery involved a sort of
passing of the torch, from bankrupt large firms to smaller companies that, because they had never been able to run up big

debts in the first place, were spared from the worst effects of the financial meltdown—and in many cases benefited from weak currencies. Indonesia was a case in point: in 1998, as the giant Suharto-era conglomerates collapsed (and the island of Java, where they had mainly been based, experienced what amounted to a depression), many small, labor-intensive businesses actually flourished; rural incomes apparently *increased* as a weak rupiah made sidelines like fish-farming increasingly profitable, and the economy apparently grew on most out islands, especially the tourist mecca of Bali.

Sooner or later, in other words, some bounce back in Asian economies was predictable, even if the fundamental situation remained troubled. But the region in general, and in particular the country that now appears most likely to show some serious economic growth in 1999—South Korea—has also been the beneficiary of some peculiar side effects of the bizarre financial events described in the last chapter.

Rube Goldberg Economics

The cartoonist Rube Goldberg was an ironic celebrant of the world of gadgets—of the ingenious devices, with their intricate moving parts, that were such a prominent part of industrial-age life. (Solid-state electronics has eliminated many of those moving parts, and hence the visibility of gadgetry in general. Think digital versus traditional watches.) The typical Rube Goldberg drawing would show an elaborate series of unlikely connections—"When sun comes up, magnifying glass burns hole in paper bag, dropping water onto ladle, opening gate, . . ."— whereby some initial cause would produce a totally unrelated effect.

Financial markets aren't supposed to work that way, and usually they don't. Money flows to where the expected profits are, and events in one part of the world are supposed to affect outcomes in another part only insofar as they change those expectations. True, when economies are vulnerable to self-fulfilling panics, there need be little if any real connection between them for crisis to spread. But there are not supposed to be arrangements of gears and camshafts that transmit financial impulses mechanically across the globe.

In the fall of 1998, however, some very strange things happened in Asian markets; and market insiders claimed that the cause was a Rube Goldberg–like linkage whereby bad news in Russia translated, through a series of odd connections, into good news for Korea.

The first few steps are the ones we already noted in the last chapter: losses by hedge funds in Russia forced them to sell assets, driving down their prices and triggering losses in other hedge funds that had made similar investments, forcing still further sales, and so on. Now, it turned out that a large part of the "short" side of many hedge fund positions consisted of borrowing in yen. The reason was that interest rates in Japan were very low, indeed virtually zero, which meant that borrowing in yen and lending in almost anything else was a sure-fire way to make money—as long as the yen didn't rise. And many investors, such as Tiger Fund's Julian Robertson, believed that the yen had nowhere to go but down. Indeed, in June of 1998 the yen had plunged to almost 150 per dollar; intervention by both the United States and Japan had arrested that decline, but after rising a bit the yen gradually slid back, and there were good economic reasons to think that the slide would continue (see the note at the end of Chapter 4).

But when the hedge funds started to lose money, other investors—including the counterparts of those yen shorts—became less willing to lend them assets. So Tiger and other hedge funds were forced to repay billions of dollars' worth of such loans. Since the loans were in yen, however, this meant that the hedge funds had to buy yen on the foreign exchange market—driving up the value of the yen. And this in turn meant further losses, because those debts suddenly became bigger in dollar terms, which forced further sales . . .

It is, of course, the same kind of circular logic we've seen so often in this book, this time operating through the liability instead of the asset side of the balance sheet. And again everyone was surprised by the power of the feedback loop. Specifically, one might have expected other investors to see the suddenly stronger yen as overvalued, and speculate against it, limiting the rise; but apparently there were not enough investors with the resources or courage to offset the tens of billions of dollars of hedge fund sales. From August to October the yen rose from 147 to the dollar to 115; a further wave of sales, this time from cash-strapped Japanese institutions forced to liquidate their dollar holdings, pushed the yen briefly above 110 in January.

But why is this good news for the rest of Asia? Because the rising yen helped pull up the currencies of Japan's neighbors, reducing the burden of dollar debt, also reducing the fear that Hong Kong or China might be forced to devalue, and thus contributing to a general recovery of financial confidence. (The plunging yen in the spring had had the opposite effect, which was why the United States helped Japan intervene to support it.)

Needless to say, this silver lining has a cloud. A strong yen may be good for Korea, but it is not at all good for Japan. On the contrary, it makes Japanese exports less competitive, reducing demand in an economy where demand is already inadequate. The economic logic saying that Japan should be following an inflationary monetary policy, which would also mean a weak yen, is if anything stronger at the time of writing than it was when the yen was near 150. This logic also means that if and when the Japanese realize that they have no other choice but to print more money, the gift they have made to their neighbors via the strong yen will be repossessed with interest. Will Korea be strong enough by then to handle the shock? Or will the Rube Goldberg device turn out to have been a time bomb?

Mahathir Opts Out

One of the truly surprising things about the rolling financial crisis of the past two years—or the past five years, if one regards the tequila and Asian crises as part of a single story—is how well the afflicted countries have behaved, how willing they have been to abide by the rules of the New World Order. For the most part governments meekly accepted the view that the crisis was a punishment for their sins, or at any rate that there was no alternative except to follow the straight and narrow until investor confidence returned. Even Malaysia's Mahathir, while avoiding becoming an IMF client, was persuaded to adopt more or less orthodox austerity policies and accept the resulting slump.

By the summer of 1998, however, his patience was wearing thin. Where was the reward for good behavior? It was a question others were asking, too. But Mahathir was in a position to do more than ask: he and his advisers began secretly planning drastic action. Like governments faced with financial crises in the past, he would impose restrictions on capital movement.

It came as an immense surprise to the world, but should not have. After all, there had been widespread talk over the course of the summer, even among respectable people, about the possibility that Asian countries might negotiate debt reschedulings—postponing repayment until their financial situations improved—or even seek debt forgiveness—a write-off of part of their obligations. (Such debt forgiveness, in the form of the Brady Plan, was exactly what put an end to the Latin American debt crisis of the 1980s.) But once you tried seriously to think through the logic of such debt reschedulings, you realized that they would tend to be ineffective as long as individuals were free to convert local currency into dollars or yen.

After all, suppose Malaysia were to try to get its economy moving by getting banks to lend more, or by spending more on public works. The constraint on such policies had been the fear that a country which tried to stimulate demand in this way would lose investor confidence—that foreign banks, for example, would get nervous and refuse to roll over their loans. So why not negotiate a "standstill" agreement with these banks? Because even with such an agreement, there would still be many other ways for the currency to come under attack. Hedge funds could still short your currency; ordinary domestic investors, fearing a devaluation, might still flee ringgit for dol-

lars. In a world of free capital mobility, merely to deal with foreign-currency debt would be to plug up only part of a rather
large hole.

But in that case, wasn't it crazy to imagine that in the modern world a government could effectively police capital flight?
Well, Mahathir had a prime counterexample: China.

Some readers may have been puzzled about the virtual
absence of China from this account of the world financial crisis. Why didn't the world's most populous country, very much
part of the Asian miracle, immediately get caught up in the crisis along with everyone else? (It may yet, as we will see below—
but so far so not-too-bad.) Were China's policies better than
those of its neighbors? Did it suffer less from the sins of crony
capitalism?

You've got to be kidding. China's economic growth has been
astonishing, but then so was the growth of everyone else in the
region until the crisis. On every other dimension China looks
worse, not better, than its neighbors: more bad banks (there
may well be no truly solvent banks in China), more nepotism,
more corruption. What spared China was the fact that, unlike
its neighbors, it had not yet made its currency "convertible":
that is, in China you still needed a government license to
change yuan into dollars, a license you would not get if your
purpose was merely to speculate against devaluation.

This lack of convertibility meant that the kind of high-speed
currency crisis experienced elsewhere, in which everyone
rushed to convert domestic currency into dollars before a devaluation, and in so doing forced that devaluation to happen,
could not happen. It also meant that, unlike its neighbors,
China remained free to print money at will. And that in turn
meant that the country was insulated from bank runs—because
people believed that the government would rush cash to threatened banks—and also that it could try to offset any slump in
demand by spending and lending more.

All of this came, of course, at a price. We saw, back in Chapter 6, how the attempt to control capital movement causes trouble: if the rules are too tight, they inhibit the "good"

transactions you want to encourage; if they are too loose, they are easily evaded. And any system where government officials are in a position to grant or refuse valuable privileges is an open invitation to corruption, an invitation many Chinese officials were delighted to accept. Recognizing these problems, China had in fact begun to discuss making its currency fully convertible—a move strongly encouraged by many in the West. Indeed, in April 1997 an IMF committee recommended that the goal of liberalizing capital accounts be formally placed into the fund's articles—that is, made an express objective of IMF policy.

In the event, of course, everyone—including the IMF—was relieved that China had not yet gotten around to freeing up capital movement. The giant nation's relative immunity to currency crisis was one of the few things that kept the Asian crisis from turning into a complete nightmare.

But if it turned out to be a good thing for China not to have freed up its capital account, why wouldn't it also be a good thing for other Asians to place restrictions on their own capital flight? Such was the reasoning of Mahathir and his advisers. And similar lines of thought were followed elsewhere. The prominent trade economist Jagdish Bhagwati had been urging capital controls for some months, beginning with a widely read article in *Foreign Affairs*. And another well-known economist came out with a call for capital controls just days before Mahathir's announcement.

I was that economist. My reasoning was exactly as described: I regarded capital controls as a bad solution, but better than the alternatives. I would have preferred less draconian controls, a clearer commitment to use the freedom gained by controls to reform as well as reflate the economy, and a declared intention to end the controls after some limited period; but I cannot dissociate myself entirely from Mahathir's economic policy. (There is no excuse for his disgusting political policy, involving trumped-up charges against former Finance Minister Anwar.)

Was Mahathir wrong (and was I)? When the controls were announced, investors declared them unworkable, proclaiming that the mad prime minister was on the road to disaster. Scare stories about how the controls would fail, or were in the process of failing, were widely circulated in the first few weeks. But so far, at least as a technical matter, the controls have worked far better than the skeptics claimed. It is still unclear whether Mahathir will be able to engineer a convincing economic recovery behind the controls; but many observers now agree that the Malaysian economy will show at least some growth this year.

But then so will several other Asian economies. It turns out that Mahathir's radical initiative was not well timed (and neither was my article). Just as Malaysia's policy went into effect, the market panic against Asian economies began to subside, at least for the time being. Partly this was the result of the Rube Goldberg linkages described above, partly a broader sense that, aside from Indonesia, Asian countries would not completely implode. Anyway, Asian currencies strengthened, interest rates came down, and things looked a little better. Was the call for capital controls alarmist? Was the IMF policy working after all?

One might have thought so; but then came a clear demonstration that the world remains a very dangerous place for developing countries, that the story is not over, and that Washington is a long way from having this problem under control as either a practical or an intellectual matter.

Bye, Bye Brazil

Brazil, goes the bitter local joke, is the country of the future — and always will be. It has a history of bursts of growth followed by disappointment, from the Amazonian rubber boom to the era of the "Brazilian miracle," the decade of 9 percent growth from 1964 to 1974. In the last two decades, the country has lurched from crisis to crisis, culminating in a near-hyperinflation as late as 1994. But Brazil, like its neighbors, became a convert to the new gospel of price stability and economic reform. In 1994 Finance Minister Fernando Henrique Cardoso introduced a new currency, the *real*, which became the centerpiece of a new drive for price stability. The success of the *real* made Cardoso immensely popular; in 1995 he became Brazil's president.

Unlike the Argentine peso, the *real* was not fixed permanently in value against the U.S. dollar. Worried that too drastic an attempt to stabilize the currency would result in Mexican-style overvaluation, Brazil's reformers instead introduced a "crawling peg"—a pre-announced series of small devaluations that would make room for a bit of lingering inflation. Initially the compromise seemed to work: inflation declined rapidly, and while some manufacturers complained that they were being priced out of world markets, the overvaluation did not seem at first to be too much of a problem. In the fall of 1997 Brazil was the subject of a speculative attack, which forced it to raise interest rates to defend the currency; this led to a slowing of growth and to some rise in unemployment; but in the early summer of 1998 the situation still looked tolerable and manageable.

Then came Russia. There may have been some direct, mechanical contagion from Russian losses: at least some hedge funds were investing in Brazil to take advantage of high interest rates, betting that the *real* would devalue only slowly, and were forced to sell out when they lost money elsewhere. But the main source of contagion seems to have been that investors suddenly thought they saw some resemblance between the two countries, mainly because Brazil also had a stubbornly high budget deficit.

There was a good case that markets were wrong in making this analogy. Brazil's economy is no Potemkin facade—on the eve of the crisis the consulting firm McKinsey came out with a study arguing, on the contrary, that the country was experiencing a surge in productivity that would dramatically raise its income over the next decade. The government was generally quite successful at collecting taxes, and did not have all that much debt outstanding. The deficit would actually have been fairly modest had the economy not been depressed and had interest payments not been so high—both of which were in large part consequences precisely of the markets' lack of confidence. But while Brazilian officials had a right to feel somewhat aggrieved, the fact was that in August the country started losing foreign exchange at an alarming rate, and something had to be done.

It wasn't just the Brazilians who were worried. Just when Asia seemed to be settling down, the IMF and the Treasury Department found themselves with the prospect of a widening crisis. And so they rushed in with a rescue plan: Brazil was supposed to be the "firewall" for the rest of the world economy.

I've already described the essentials of that plan (back in Chapter 6). It was, to repeat, almost a caricature of the plans followed in Asia: raise taxes, cut spending, keep interest rates high, and wait for something to improve. It was apparent from the start that this was a plan guaranteed to produce a severe recession. (At the time of writing, many analysts were predicting that the Brazilian economy would shrink more than 5 percent in 1999; Brazil's potential output, the amount that it could produce at a normal unemployment rate, is probably *growing* at least 5 percent per year. So this is in effect a forecast that output will fall more than 10 percent below what the economy could produce.) It was also apparent that Brazil's politicians were being asked to do something extraordinary: to impose drastic austerity measures on constituents already being battered by economic slump, and to do so with no clear expectation that this sacrifice would receive any reward other than a possible remission of speculative pressure.

It was no surprise, then, that Cardoso had trouble getting his fiscal measures through Congress. It was a bit more of a surprise when the governor of one of Brazil's states, who happened to be a former president, declared that he could no longer pay the money Minas Gerais owed the central government, and had his internal debt moratorium upheld by the courts. This turned out to be the event that triggered the *real* crisis of January 1999. But the truth is that it is hard to see how the plan could have worked.

The crisis was still unfolding as this was written. But even the preliminary stages of the breakdown of the Brazilian plan carried some lessons.

Here is a timetable of the crisis:

- January 7: The former president Itamar Franco, governor of Minas Gerais, declares that he will no longer pay his state's debts to the central government. The announcement starts a process of capital flight from Brazil, draining reserves at the rate of about $1 billion per day.

- January 13: The head of Brazil's central bank resigns, and the government devalues the *real*—but by only 8 percent, repeating the same mistake made in Mexico and in Russia. (That is, the devaluation signaled that the exchange rate commitment was gone, but was not enough to satisfy the markets.)

- January 15: The central bank stops intervening in the markets and lets the *real* float. The market reaction is surprisingly favorable: the currency drops only 10 percent, much less than pundits expected—and the Brazilian stock market surges an amazing 33 percent, apparently believing that the end of the currency peg will allow the government to cut interest rates and engineer an economic recovery. Has a Third World country finally managed a successful devaluation?

- January 16–17: Brazilian officials fly to Washington and meet with IMF and Treasury officials, who insist that despite the good news on Friday interest rates must be raised, not lowered, to stabilize the currency.

- January 18: The government announces that interest rates will not be reduced; the immediate result is despondency, and the *real* plunges. It declines day after day. On Sunday *Fôlha de São Paulo*, one of the country's most influential newspapers, calls for "centralization of foreign exchange trading," that is, temporary capital controls. By January 28 the *real* is trading at 2.10 to the dollar, compared with 1.22 before the initial devaluation.

It is a sad story; it also raises some agonizing questions.

Surely one big mystery is why officials in Washington demanded, on that crucial first weekend after the *real* was floated, that Brazil raise interest rates. The currency seemed to have stabilized spontaneously; why not give it a chance? Anyway, there was a good case to be made that Brazil, unlike Asian countries, could accept even a substantial depreciation of its currency without too much damage. Unlike Korean companies, Brazilian firms were not highly leveraged, with lots of dollar debt; so a weakened *real* would not push them into bankruptcy. The only concern would be inflation: would the decline in the *real* set off a surge in prices? Imports are only 7 percent of Brazil's GDP, so the direct impact would be small; only if workers demanded wage increases, and companies passed along those increases in prices, would there be a problem. And given the already depressed state of the Brazilian economy, how likely was it that workers would risk their jobs by making such demands?

It would certainly have been risky to leave interest rates unchanged or even cut them and see what happened. However, it was equally risky to raise them; and why not at least wait a few days to see whether it was necessary?

What seems to have happened is that Washington officials had become so committed to the idea that one must always raise interest rates to defend the currency that they could not bring themselves to consider the alternative. Perhaps at some level there was also an element of self-justification involved. If it turned out that Brazil could get away with floating its currency, if raising rates was not essential, then maybe all the pain being inflicted under typical IMF plans was unnecessary — maybe they had imposed those harsh recessions gratuitously. It cannot have been a pleasant thought, and perhaps that thought made the officials unwilling to allow Brazil to try the experiment.

But if the intention was to vindicate the policies of the past, the effect was just the opposite. Indeed, Brazil's crisis had the feel of a recurrent nightmare: once again, as in Mexico, Thailand, Indonesia, and Korea, a seemingly successful economy had gone to Washington in its hour of need, tried its best to follow the plan Washington devised, and been rewarded with a catastrophe. At the time of writing, J. P. Morgan was forecasting a 5 percent decline in Brazil's GDP, Salomon 6 percent; while these forecasts will surely be revised, it seems clear that Brazil is now set for a crisis at least as bad as Thailand's or Korea's.

Who's Next?

Have we run out of vulnerable economies, or are there still more crises to come?

Three rather distinct groups of economies have not yet had full-scale crises, and still could. Think of them as the good, the bad, and the wealthy.

The good economies are those that have tried from the beginning to live under the rules of the New World Order, that have had sound money and sound budgets, but may nonetheless find themselves dragged down by the backwash from their neighbors' crises. In Asia, Hong Kong is the prime example, with its exemplary budgetary and monetary discipline, its careful bank regulation, counting for naught when the economies around it are devaluing and imploding. Things in Hong Kong could still get much worse. Hong Kong's Latin counterpart is Argentina, whose currency board may not save it from crisis as its biggest neighbor's currency and economy plunge. At the time of writing, Argentina is talking about taking the ultimate step to assure currency credibility: giving up the peso and adopting the U.S. dollar. But even Argentina still has some pride; this would take time that the country may not have; and even a dollarized economy can still have collapsing banks and bankrupt companies. And other basically well-run emerging markets around the world, from Mexico to Israel, are feeling the chill wind; who knows which may catch cold?

The bad are those economies that deserve a crisis at least as much as those already afflicted, but have thus far managed to avoid being caught up in the maelstrom—usually because they have not played by the rules. The prime example is, of course, China—corrupt, crony-ridden, with terrible banks, but saved so far by its inconvertible currency.

Could China go the way of its neighbors? Possibly: but the crisis would look a bit different, because of the capital controls and the absence of large foreign-currency debts. One scenario would involve massive domestic bank runs—with the government hesitant to provide the huge injections of cash needed to stop the runs, for fear that putting too much money into circulation would create such an incentive to swap yuan for dollars that the currency controls would prove ineffective. The other scenario would involve a sort of Japanese-style slowdown in domestic spending, which the government is again unable to fight effectively, not because the interest rate is zero but because rates can go only so low before, once again, causing capital flight that swamps the controls. In both cases the crisis story builds on a real problem: China's banks really are a mess, and the country does have flagging private investment and consumer spending.

The good news is that the Chinese government is well aware of these risks and is trying to combat them through massive public investment spending, a classic Keynesian remedy. There clearly is significant capital flight from China despite the controls, but it is a steady leakage rather than a torrent, and the country's immense foreign exchange reserves are still intact. The clear and present danger (I think: anyone who is confident about such things after the last two years has not been paying attention) is not that China itself will collapse, but that—as it perceives the pressure gradually increasing—it will choose to devalue its currency. This would not lead to a catastrophe for China (remember those capital controls), but would endanger whatever recovery is taking place elsewhere in Asia.

Finally, there are the wealthy: the nations of the First World. Are we vulnerable?

Japan is already in deep trouble. At the time of writing, officials there were predicting recovery, based on the slight upturn in the fourth quarter of 1998—a consequence of massive public works spending that most outside observers think cannot be sustained. (In an embarrassingly naked display of wishful thinking, those same officials have lately taken to predicting imminent catastrophe for the United States.) I believe that Japan remains deep in its liquidity trap and that only a radical change of policy can get it out.

The question therefore is whether Europe and the United States may find themselves in similar straits. And the answer is that if it can happen to Japan, it can happen to us. It's easy to tell stories about how we can all turn Japanese. Europe's growth is slowing, and it is very close to actual deflation; what happens if the European Central Bank waits until that deflation has become embedded in inflation before cutting interest rates? The United States stock market is at levels that seem extremely hard to justify; can a crash depress consumer demand so much that the Fed cannot offset its effects?

But these are scenarios, not predictions. Indeed they may even be self-denying prophecies; for if we understand the old-fashioned hazards that have reemerged under the New World Order, we may be able to avoid them.

■

The Return of

Depression Economics

THE world economy is not in depression; it probably will not be in depression anytime soon. But while depression itself has not returned, depression economics—the kinds of problems that characterized much of the world economy in the 1930s, but have not been seen since—has staged a stunning comeback. Five years ago hardly anybody thought that modern nations would be forced to endure bone-crushing recessions for fear of currency speculators; that a major advanced country could find itself persistently unable to generate enough spending to keep its workers and factories employed; that even the Federal Reserve would worry about its ability to counter a financial-market panic. The world economy has turned out to be a much more dangerous place than we imagined.

How did the world become this dangerous? More important, how can we make it safer? In this book I have told many stories; now it is time to try to draw some morals.

What Is Depression Economics?

What does it mean to say that depression economics has returned? Essentially it means that for the first time in two generations, failures on the demand side of the economy—insufficient private spending to make use of the available productive capacity—have become the clear and present limitation on prosperity for a large part of the world.

We—by which I mean economists, but also policymakers and the educated public at large—weren't ready for this. The specific set of silly ideas that has laid claim to the name "supply-side economics" is a crank doctrine, which would have little influence if it did not appeal to the prejudices of editors and wealthy men; but over the past few decades there has been a steady drift in emphasis in economic thinking away from the demand side to the supply side of the economy.

This drift was partly the result of theoretical disputes within economics, which—as they so often do—gradually filtered out, in somewhat garbled form, into wider discourse. Briefly, the source of the theoretical disputes was this: in principle shortfalls of overall demand would cure themselves if only wages and prices fell rapidly in the face of unemployment. In the story of the depressed baby-sitting co-op, one way the situation could have resolved itself would have been for the price of an hour of baby-sitting in terms of coupons to fall, so that the purchasing power of the existing supply of coupons would have risen, and the co-op would have returned to "full employment" without any action by its management. In reality this doesn't happen or, if it does, takes a very long time; but economists have been unable to agree about exactly why. The result has been a series of bitter academic battles that have made the whole subject of recessions and how they happen a sort of professional minefield, in which ever fewer economists dare to tread; and the public has understandably concluded either that economists don't understand recessions or that demand-side remedies have been discredited. The truth is that good old-fashioned demand-side macroeconomics has a lot to offer in our current predicament—but its defenders lack all conviction, while its critics are filled with a passionate intensity.

Paradoxically, if the theoretical weaknesses of demand-side economics are one reason we were unready for the return of depression-type issues, its practical successes are another. During all the decades that economists have argued with one another over whether monetary policy can actually be used to get an economy out of a recession, central banks have repeatedly gone ahead and done it—done it so effectively that the idea of a prolonged economic slump due to insufficient demand became implausible. Surely the Federal Reserve and its counterparts in other countries could always cut interest rates enough to keep spending high; except in the very short run, then, the only limitation on economic performance was an economy's ability to produce—that is, the supply side.

Even now, many economists still think of recessions as a minor issue, their study as a faintly disreputable subject; the trendy work has all been concerned with technological progress and long-run growth. These are fine, important questions, and in the long run they are what really matter—but as Keynes pointed out, in the long run we are all dead.

Meanwhile, in the short run the world is lurching from crisis to crisis, all of them crucially involving the problem of generating sufficient demand. Japan is finding that conventional monetary and fiscal policies aren't enough; if it can happen to Japan, how sure can we be that the European economy or even the still-booming economy of the United States will not find itself in the same trap? Mexico, Thailand, Malaysia, Indonesia, Korea, Brazil: one developing country after another has experienced a recession that at least temporarily undoes years of economic progress, and finds that the conventional policy responses only make things worse. Once again, the question of how to keep demand adequate to make use of the economy's capacity has become crucial. Depression economics is back.

What Is at Stake?

The most immediate risk from the return of depression economics is, of course, the possibility that the malaise will spread—that Argentina, or South Africa, or Turkey, or (God help us) China will be added to the list of casualties; that deflation in Europe or a stock market crash in the United States will create Japanese-style conditions across the advanced world as a whole. Even if the damage is contained, however, more subtle risks to economic progress remain, because generally free markets, with all the benefits they bring, are unlikely to survive in a world where insufficient demand is a continual threat.

Remember the Keynesian compact. The free-market faithful tend to think of Keynesian policies broadly defined—of deliberate efforts by the government to stimulate demand—as the enemy of what they stand for. But they are wrong, for in a world where there is often not enough demand to go around, the case for free markets is a hard case to make.

Let's be concrete and consider the case of Argentina. Assume that Argentina's currency board survives, or perhaps even that the country abandons its peso altogether and dollarizes—but that, as seems all too likely, it suffers a serious recession and faces the prospect of years of high unemployment. Now imagine that a powerful union or business group demands that the Argentine government protect jobs with tariffs or import quotas. The conventional response to such demands is to say that they are not really about creating jobs, only about shifting them around: a tariff can add employment in one industry, but at least as many jobs will be lost elsewhere as a result. And this is surely true in the United States, where the inflationary pressures created by protectionism for some industries would force the Federal Reserve to raise interest rates and thereby crowd out as many or more jobs in others. But in a country that has high unemployment because of inadequate demand and that cannot do anything to increase demand, because it fears capital flight, this argument is simply wrong. Right now a tariff *would* increase employment in Argentina, and to pretend otherwise is intellectually dishonest. This does not mean that Argentina— or Israel, or Hong Kong, or any of the many other economies in somewhat similar positions—should become protectionist; but it does mean that we had better start trying to find ways to get them back to more or less full employment, or the rationale for free-market policies is going to start to wear increasingly thin.

Again, the right perspective is to realize how very much good free markets in general, and the rise of globalization in particular, have done the human race; the point is to preserve and extend those gains. Now as in the 1930s, however, one cannot defend globalization merely by repeating free-market mantras, even as economy after economy crashes. If we want to see more economic miracles, more nations making the transition from abject poverty to the hope of a decent life, we had better find answers to the newly intractable problems of depression economics.

Blaming the Victim

Even now, there are still many pundits who do not accept the idea that the recent string of economic crises demonstrates a problem with the system. Instead, they point to the weaknesses of the individual countries, to the policy mistakes of their leaders. Japan's banks were too careless, Indonesia's ruler too corrupt, Brazil's budget deficits too large. Follow the right policies, and you will do just fine. And there is no question that each country that has found itself suffering from the problems of depression economics, even if it was widely praised for its management before things went wrong (and most of these countries were), turns out on closer examination to have serious flaws. But one needs to be careful about what inferences to draw.

Imagine a stretch of highway that has recently been the scene of an unusual number of accidents. Investigators look closely into the causes of each accident and in almost every case find some precipitating factor: the driver had had too much to drink, his tires were bald, he reacted wrongly to a skid, and so on. Their conclusion is that there is nothing wrong with the road; the problem lies with the drivers. But this conclusion is doubly biased. First, almost every driver or car will, if scrutinized closely enough, turn out to be flawed in some way; are these drivers any worse than average? Second, even if they are unusually bad drivers, this does not absolve the road: good drivers are less likely to have accidents on any road, but good roads do not demand perfection of their users.

Similarly, a good economic system should not require perfect policies of its denizens. It is striking how many of the nations that have suffered most in recent years, from Japan to Korea, were placed on pedestals not long ago; granted that their former admirers were excessively starstruck, were they really as badly run as people now suppose? Or is this all a matter of ex post facto rationalization? Put it this way: if the United States, which has thus far been almost giddily prosperous as Asia and Latin America are pummeled, were to falter, we can be quite sure that after the fact pundits would explain at great length why we deserved our fate. *Of course* those unregulated hedge funds, the entry of ill-informed small investors into the high-stakes game of day trading, the over-availability of consumer credit and the resulting zero savings rate were disasters waiting to happen.

What is particularly poignant about the economic crises of the last two years is that by and large the countries caught up in them were, by all accounts, following *better* policies than they had in the past. As one despondent Brazilian put it, "Brazil has never had such a responsible government; the environment has never been better for business; why is this happening to us?" And this was before January's catastrophe.

The urge to blame the victim comes in several guises. One is what I think of as the "hangover theory," the view that recessions are a deserved, indeed necessary punishment for previous excesses. Japan is paying the price now (eight years later!) for the speculative excesses of its "bubble economy" and Asia for the borrow-and-spend boom of the 1990s; and there is nothing for it but, as Schumpeter said in the 1930s, to let "the work of depression" proceed. The hangover theory is peculiarly appealing not because it offers easy answers but because it doesn't; it gives its adherents the pleasure of moralizing with a clear conscience, secure in the belief that they are not being heartless—they are practicing tough love.

But the theory is utterly wrong. Excesses there were; many investments will have to be written off, even if the economies recover. There is no good reason, however, why misguided investments in the past should leave perfectly good workers unemployed, perfectly useful factories idle. If the U.S. stock market should crash tomorrow, nobody would expect Alan Greenspan to shield stockholders from their losses; but we would and should accuse him of malfeasance if he did not do everything possible to keep those paper losses from causing mass unemployment.

A related temptation is the tendency to regard an economic downturn as evidence that the economy has "structural" problems that must be resolved before it can recover—and even to say that it would be wrong to try to stimulate demand and generate a recovery, because this would reduce the pressure for change. Japan's economic model, we are told, has failed: its managers are too hidebound, its corporations insufficiently bottom-line-oriented, its banks too chummy with their clients. No wonder it is stagnating; a severe recession, which will shake up the system, is actually good for Japan's future. (A normally very sensible Japanese economist told me, "Your proposal would only let these guys continue with business as usual, just when they are finally starting to change.") But not all major problems are structural—sometimes all a stalled car needs is a jump start—and while we all have structural problems, you can make a good case that prosperity rather than depression is the best environment in which to cure them.

Finally, let us take care not to define success down. Until Brazil blew up in January, officials in Washington and elsewhere were starting to exhibit a peculiar smugness. Korea seemed to be over the worst; Japan was showing signs of a bit of growth; see, their policies were working. This was like saying that the high-way-safety program works because most accident victims do survive and even manage to walk again. We have a long way to go before we can claim to have ended the resurgence of depression economics.

So what should we be doing differently?

Protecting the Rich

The world is an unfair place. Wealthy countries tend to be blessed on all counts. Not only are they rich, but they generally have stable and effective governments. And they fall on the good side of the double standard: investors and markets tend to be willing to give them the benefit of the doubt. All this gives them a freedom of action, an ability to cope with economic problems, that poorer nations can only envy.

Nonetheless, Japan has shown us that even an advanced nation can get stuck; the scary events of last fall suggest that advanced countries remain at some risk of runaway financial crises. What can they do to protect themselves?

I've already made it clear what I believe Japan should do (Chapter 4): having gotten stuck in its liquidity trap—unable to recover by means of conventional monetary policy, because even a zero interest rate is not low enough—having exhausted its ability to spend its way out with budget deficits, Japan must now radically expand its money supply, with the aim of convincing savers and investors that its current deflation will turn into sustained though modest inflation. Once the Japanese make up their mind to do this, the results will startle them; but it will take time for them to accept the idea that such a radical step is the only way out.

The United States and Europe are not currently in liquidity traps, so their concern must be how to avoid getting into one. The most obvious precautionary measure is to make sure that

inflation does not get too low when times are good: to set a target rate of at least 2 percent, so that real interest rates can be
reduced to minus 2 rather than merely to zero if the situation
demands. By that standard the United States was doing more or
less the right thing at the time of writing, but European monetary policy is far too conservative: growth was slowing, inflation
was less than 1 percent and declining, and the interest rate, at
3 percent, was too low to give a comfortable margin for future
recession fighting. I hope that by the time this book comes out
the European Central Bank will have moved aggressively to cut
rates and stimulate growth; if it does not, the liquidity trap
could be about to claim another victim.

Over the longer term, it would be a good idea to try to reduce
some of the vulnerabilities exposed by recent market events.
The hedge fund scare revealed that modern financial markets,
by creating many institutions that perform bank-like functions
but do not benefit from bank-type safety nets, have in effect
reinvented the possibility of traditional financial panics. Let's
try to figure out who owes what to whom, and build some new
firewalls, before crisis hits again.

Finally, if crisis does strike, the rule is simple: cut interest
rates drastically, without hesitation. Although Greenspan clearly believes that U.S. stocks are overvalued, I hope and believe
that he would not make the mistake the Japanese made when
their own bubble burst, that of welcoming the correction and
waiting to cut interest rates until it was too late. I am less sure
about the European Central Bank; let us hope its directors
understand the stakes.

On the whole, I have an easy conscience about the problems
of the advanced countries. What I mean by that statement is
that the solutions for these problems do not seem to involve any
especially painful trade-offs. There is, in particular, no economic evidence suggesting that inflation at the 2 percent rate
that seems appropriate for Europe and the United States, or
even the 4 percent rate I believe Japan should target, does any
noticeable harm; and the things advanced countries need to do

to counter depression economics do not involve any compromise of the commitment to free markets.

The trade-offs facing developing countries, by contrast, seem more difficult.

Helping the Poor

As this final chapter was being written, fur was flying at Davos, site of that usually self-congratulatory winter soiree for the world's elite. Everyone was blaming the IMF for the disaster in Brazil, calling for the resignation of its managing director and even the abolition of the institution itself. But the critics disagreed with each other, it seemed, even more than they did with IMF policies. Some argued that Brazil should have fixed the value of the *real* permanently, once and for all, by instituting an Argentine-style currency board. Others argued that the currency should have been allowed to float freely, that the crucial mistake was raising interest rates to support it. And some, of course, were arguing that Brazil should have instituted capital controls to limit speculation.

The peculiar thing is that all of the critics could, to some extent, be right. Arguably the IMF's policy—which defends the exchange rate at enormous cost, but which neither provides a credible promise that the defense will succeed nor imposes restrictions on those who would speculate on its failure— achieves the worst of all worlds. A clear choice of *any* of the alternatives—a freely floating exchange rate, a currency board, or a regime of capital controls—might be better than sitting somewhere in the middle.

That said, I am skeptical of the currency board option. To repeat what I said in Chapter 6, even if it works, such a board protects a country from speculation against its currency, but not from speculation against its economy; perhaps the risks are less, but this is far from certain. And if a currency board fails— which it will unless the political conditions for its success are very favorable—the result will be a truly terrible catastrophe, which leaves the government with no credibility at all.

The next option is to give devaluation a chance: to let the markets push your currency down, without raising interest rates. This works for advanced countries; maybe it will work in some developing countries too. What seems painfully clear from events in Brazil is that the contrary strategy, of raising interest rates to sky-high levels in an attempt to keep money from fleeing, is a losing strategy on all counts. Not only does it send the real economy into a deadly skid; by feeding investors' sense of doom, it often fails even to stabilize the exchange rate. It seems quite possible that if Brazil had not raised interest rates to defend the *real*, the currency would actually have avoided its subsequent plunge. It's true that some of the Asian countries that tried the high-interest-rate policy are now starting to recover; well, most accidents are not fatal.

But what if devaluation is unacceptable, because companies have large foreign debts or because the public too easily loses faith in the currency? Then it is hard to see how to avoid the conclusion that capital controls become necessary, as a sort of curfew on capital flight while calm is restored. Many free-market advocates will react with horror to the very idea: they believe that the right to put their money where they see fit is a sacrosanct principle. But just as the right to free speech does not necessarily include the right to shout "Fire!" in a crowded theater, the principle of free markets does not necessarily mean that investors must be allowed to trample each other in a stampede. For that is what happens in a runaway crisis. Brazil would be a quite safe place to invest, were it not for the risk of crisis — that is, it would be safe for each investor if he were sure that other investors were not about to take flight. But investors mistrusted *each other* — and the crisis came.

The point is that when crisis threatens it may well be in the interest not only of the country but *even of investors* to impose emergency capital controls — just as the population of an earthquake-ravaged city is better off if the government imposes a temporary curfew. One might even argue that the expectation that such controls would be imposed if necessary, instead of discouraging long-term investors from coming, would actually reassure them, at least once they get used to the idea.

Perhaps a quick way to summarize this advice is with the old injunction to go to the church of your choice, but go, dammit. In a financial crisis a government must do something decisive. Institute a currency board if that seems feasible and you are prepared to live with the long-term implications; or let the currency float if you think that can work in your country; or impose emergency capital controls quickly. Whatever you do, don't dither.

Still, the best thing would certainly be to prevent crises in the first place. What can be done? Nowadays everyone is in favor of better information, more "transparency" in the accounts of banks and companies, closer regulation of financial risk-taking, and so on. By all means let's do all that. Beyond this, we need to find ways to reduce the strength of the feedback loops described in Chapter 5. Since we are talking about long-run measures here, there is still time for discussion; my own suggestion is that governments actively try to discourage local companies from borrowing in foreign currencies, and also perhaps from relying too much on borrowed funds in general (that is, reduce their "leverage"). The best way to do this is probably by taxing companies that borrow in foreign currency. In so doing, countries might regain the ability to allow their currencies to slide without provoking a financial collapse and, in so doing, head off future crises at the pass.

I don't like the idea that countries will need to interfere in markets—that they will have to limit the free market in order to save it. But it is hard to see how anyone who has been paying attention can still insist that nothing of the kind needs to be done, that financial markets will always reward virtue and punish only vice.

Pride and Prejudice

A few days before this was written, a desperate President Cardoso rejected the idea of capital controls, insisting that to impose them would be to give up Brazil's hopes of ever becoming a "first-class" nation. This statement came as financial newsletters were speculating that Brazil might default on its debt, even declare a bank holiday, and as forecasters were scrambling to increase their estimates of the prospective slump in the country's output.

One cannot help feeling sorry for Cardoso, who tried to do all the right things and received no reward for his efforts. The apparent discovery that Brazil was not ready to swim in the world capital market without a life preserver was a terrible humiliation. Yet his country cannot afford to stand too much on its pride. It needs a way out of its dilemma, and if that way out requires capital controls, so be it. After all, most of those "first-class" nations had capital controls themselves for a generation after World War II; they became prosperous and then opened themselves up to free capital movement, not the other way around.

The truth is that pride is a luxury none of us can afford in a world that has turned out to pose unsuspected risks. If, as rumor has it, some of the opposition to monetary expansion in Japan comes from officials who feel diminished by a weak yen, who fear that they will be eclipsed now that the euro has become the main rival to the dollar, they should be ashamed of themselves. It is on the other hand very good news that European officials, who not long ago seemed to view a strong euro as the most important goal of their new monetary union, are now talking about the primary importance of maintaining employment and avoiding deflation.

Even more important than pride as an obstacle to sensible action, however, is prejudice — by which I mean the adherence of too many influential people to orthodox views about economic policy that are no longer relevant to our changed world. Twenty years ago, when even advanced countries were suffering from double-digit inflation, when intrusive foreign exchange control was a source of major economic distortions and widespread corruption, to preach the virtues of price stability and currency convertibility was clearly to move the world in the right direction. But we are no longer living in that world, and the useful rallying cries of one era have become the dangerous shibboleths of another. To refuse to reconsider the appropriateness of zero inflation when your country is in or near a liquidity trap, to refuse to contemplate capital controls when investors' fears of economic collapse are turning into self-fulfilling prophecy, is to value the appearance of sound economic policy over the reality.

Anyone who spends much time trying to debate economics outside the confines of the academy quickly develops both a thick skin and a cynical outlook. Nonetheless, there is something shocking about the mental inflexibility of many influential people, not just government officials but also journalists and even professional economists. Economic analysis is not, or at any rate is not supposed to be, a set of rules to be followed on all occasions; rather, it is supposed to be a way of thinking, something that allows you to craft new responses to an ever-changing world. What keeps it useful is precisely the fact that old models can be taught new tricks—that a basic understanding of how, say, recessions happen tells you how to get out of a slump that does not respond to the usual treatment. But in the last year I have been struck by how many people reverse the process, hastily cobbling together new models to justify old tricks. Those who worried about balanced budgets back when uncontrollable deficits were the problem suddenly insist that raising taxes and cutting spending will actually prevent a recession, because it will improve confidence. Those who wanted stable prices back when inflation was the risk now claim that "managed inflation" will somehow backfire, because in Japan—though nowhere else in the world—a weaker currency and lower real interest rates will actually reduce demand. If such arguments were made on behalf of *unorthodox* policies, they would rightly be dismissed as nonsense; but it seems that ad hockery in the defense of orthodoxy is no vice.

And this brings us to the deepest sense in which depression economics has returned. The quintessential economic sentence is supposed to be "There is no free lunch"; it says that there are limited resources, that to have more of one thing you must accept less of another, that there is no gain without pain. Depression economics, however, is the study of situations where there *is* a free lunch, if we can only figure out how to get our hands on it, because there are unemployed resources that could be put to work. In 1930 John Maynard Keynes wrote that "we have involved ourselves in a colossal muddle, having blundered in the control of a delicate machine, the working of which we do not understand." The true scarcity in his world—and ours—was therefore not of resources, or even of virtue, but of understanding.

We will not achieve the understanding we need, however, unless we are willing to think clearly about our problems and to follow those thoughts wherever they lead. Some people say that the problems of Japan, of emerging Asia, of Brazil are structural, with no quick cure available; but I believe that the only important structural obstacles to world prosperity are the obsolete doctrines that clutter the minds of men.

Index

Index

McKinsey company, 147
Mahathir Mohamad, xii, 123,
    128, 142–44
  capital controls sought by,
    145–46
  conspiracy theory of, 99,
    124–25
Major, John, 123
Malaysia, 33, 34, 35, 87, 106, 107,
    128, 143, 145–46, 156
  Asian financial crisis and,
    96–97, 98, 123–24, 125
managed inflation, 76–81, 167
Marshall, Alfred, 77
Marxism, 3
Medley Report, 131
Mellon, Andrew, vii
Menem, Carlos, 46–47
Mexico, 17, 26, 40–45, 47, 48–57,
    69, 85, 87, 88, 92, 95,
    111, 138, 149, 150, 151,
    156
  bailout of, 56–57, 59
  Brady Plan and, 43–44, 48, 53
  Chiapas uprising in, 51
  NAFTA and, 44–45, 51
  political system of, 42–43
  tequila crisis and, 39–40,
    52–56
  trade deficit of, 48–49
  Washington Consensus
    Reforms in, 42
"Mexico: Stabilization, Reform,
    and No Growth" (Dorn-
    busch), 50
MITI (Ministry of International
    Trade and Industry),
    Japanese, 62–63, 64
Monetary Authority, Hong Kong,
    126–28

"Monetary Theory and the Great
    Capitol Hill Baby-sitting
    Co-op Crisis" (Sweeney
    and Sweeney), 8–11
"money multiplier" process, 86
moral hazard, 66–68, 88, 101,
    134, 136
"Myth of Asia's Miracle, The"
    (Krugman), 32

Nehru, Jawaharlal, 15–16
neoclassical synthesis, 103
Nixon, Richard M., 12
North American Free Trade
    Agreement (NAFTA),
    44–45, 51, 56

Peregrine Investment Holdings,
    89
Perón, Juan, 46–47
Perot, Ross, 51
peso, Argentinian, 47–48, 54–55,
    147, 157
peso, Mexican, 48–49, 51, 52, 53,
    56, 57
Philippines, 16
Pinochet, Augusto, 39
Poland, 4
Potemkin, Grigori Aleksan-
    drovich, 129
pound, British, 50, 93
  devaluation of, 122–24
PRI (Institutional Revolutionary
    Party), Mexican, 40, 42,
    43, 51–52

Quantum Fund, 120, 122, 124,
    125, 126

Reagan, Ronald, 3, 54, 93

Index

real, Brazilian, 137, 163, 164
 devaluation of, 111–12,
  148–50
 introduction of, 146–47
 1999 crisis of, 148–50
recession, 7–12, 72, 106, 126, 148,
  154, 156, 167
 accelerator principle and,
  138–39
 hangover theory of, 159–60
 onset of Asian, 92–93
 recovering from, 11–12, 74–75,
  103
ringgit, Malaysian, 108, 143–44
Robertson, Julian, 126, 141
Rostow, Walt Whitman, 22
ruble, Russian, 131
rupiah, Indonesian, 96, 110, 140
Russia, ix, 4, 5, 26, 111, 133, 141,
  147, 149
 nuclear arsenal of, 130–31
 transition to capitalism in,
  129–32
Russia, Imperial, 129

Sachs, Jeffrey, 116, 117
Salinas de Gortari, Carlos, 39, 42,
  43, 44, 51
Samuelson, Paul, 103
Schumpeter, Joseph, 12, 160
Schwartz, Peter, 7
Serra Puche, Jaime, 53
"short" positions, 119–20
Singapore, 23, 31–32, 33, 34, 35
socialism, 129
 collapse of, 2–5
Solow, Robert, 29, 36
Soros, George, xi, 50, 99, 124,
  125, 127, 131, 134
 British pound's devaluation

 and, 121–23
South Africa, Republic of, viii,
  157
Soviet Union, 16, 18, 32, 34, 61
 collapse of, 3–5, 6, 31
 TFP of, 30–31
Stalin, Joseph, 18, 61
stock market crash of 1929, vii
stock market crash of 1987, 13
Suharto, 99
Summers, Lawrence, 78
supply-side economics, 155
Sweden, 52, 65
Sweeney, Joan, 10–11
Sweeney, Richard, 8, 10–11

Taiwan, 18, 23, 33
"Tale of Two Cities, A" (Young),
  31–32
technical efficiency change,
  32–33
technology, 13–15, 34
 economic growth and, 27–28
 globalization and, 16
 labor productivity and, 27–28
tequila crisis, 52–58, 87, 92, 142
 Argentina as affected by,
  39–40, 54–58
 Mexico and, 39–40, 52–56
Thailand, ix, x–xi, 33, 35, 83–95,
  111, 115, 125, 150–51,
  156
 crisis of July 2, 1997 in, 89–90
 and devaluation of baht, 83,
  91–93, 95
 economic boom in, 84–89
 onset of recession in, 92–95,
  97, 100
 trade deficit of, 87–88
Third World, 15–19, 23, 84

Third World (*continued*)
  as "emerging markets," 84–85
Tiger Fund, 126, 141
Time, 124
total factor productivity (TFP),
    27–32, 33
  of Soviet Union, 30–31
Treasury Department, U.S., 56,
    58, 59, 103, 114, 148,
    149
Tsang, Donald, xii, 128–29
Turkey, 157
"Tyranny of Numbers, The"
    (Young), 32

unemployment, 12, 19, 69, 155,
    157
United States, ix, x, xiii, 7, 13, 19,
    23, 24, 28–29, 53, 76,
    77, 100, 104, 107, 111,
    113, 116, 120, 138, 141,
    142, 156, 157, 159
  avoidance of liquidity trap by,
    161–62
  Mexican bailout by, 56–57, 59
  NAFTA and, 44
  Russian economic reform and,
    130–31
  savings and loan affair in, 68

vulnerability to recession of, 153

Vogel, Ezra, 62

Washington Consensus, 42
Weber, Max, 36
Wired, 7, 13, 15
Woodstock conference, 96, 97–98
World Bank, xi, 1, 32–33, 35, 41,
    56–57, 85, 103
World Competitiveness Report of
    1994, 39
World Financial Crisis, The
    (Soros), xi
World War II, 103, 166

Yeltsin, Boris, 130
yen, Japanese, 78, 85, 98, 108,
    127, 166
  baht's relationship to, 86–87,
    90
  exchange rate and, 80–81
  managed inflation and, 79–82
  rise of, 141–42
Yom Kippur War of 1973, viii
Young, Alwyn, 31–32, 34
yuan, Chinese, 144, 152

Zedillo, Ernesto, 51–52, 59